The
Carter Family
Scrapbook

(Ratshoon)

The Carter Family Scrapbook

An Intimate Close-up of America's First Family

by
James Neyland

Grosset & Dunlap

A Filmways Company

Publishers New York

Contents

Acknowledgments

This book would not have been possible if it had not been for the indulgence and generosity of Mrs. Lillian Carter, of Plains, Georgia. Not only did she provide information and introductions to others, but she took time to read proofs and point out errors. She also freely opened her family photo albums and permitted me to photograph their contents. Most important, however, were her moral support and encouragement. My gratitude to her extends far beyond the creation of this book; words cannot express what her friendship has meant to me.

I am also grateful to Gloria Carter Spann for taking time out of her busy schedule to offer advice, information, and criticism. She has been a friend as well as a critic. My thanks also extend to Walter Spann, who remained patient and smiling throughout.

Other members of the Carter family have been extremely helpful and friendly. I wish to thank Ruth Carter Stapleton for slowing up long enough for me to get to know and like her. I thank Billy and Sybil Carter and their children for treating me as a member of the family. I thank Jimmy and Rosalynn Carter and members of their family—Jeff and Annette, Chip and Caron, and Amy—for allowing me to share their Christmas celebrations.

I am grateful, too, to members of Rosalynn's family, particularly her mother, Mrs. Allie Smith, who graciously permitted me to photograph her personal collection of family pictures and who supplied me with considerable information about the Murray and Smith families. She also introduced me to Mrs. Beth Walters, who provided the Murray genealogy, and to Mrs. Teresa Smith, who gave me the Smith genealogy.

Information about the Carter and Gordy genealogies was supplied by Ken Thomas, whose article on the subject appeared in the Winter 1976 issue of *Georgia Life*. I am grateful to him and to Mrs. Ann Lewis, editor of that magazine, for allowing me to use this information.

I have had considerable assistance from the staff at Grosset & Dunlap. Editor-in-chief Bob Markel has gone above and beyond the call of duty in offering his help; and I am grateful to editors Grace Shaw and Sylvie Reice for their work on the manuscript and on the selection of photographs. Alyss Dorese, Erik Larson, and Chris Breen have also been of great help to me. I especially want to thank Diana Price for her unruffled cooperation in times of stress.

It is impossible to thank all the many people in Plains, Americus, and Atlanta, Georgia, who offered their assistance. But I do want to express my gratitude to Maxine Reese, whose graciousness and good humor make her the best public relations representative any town could have; to Ralph and Dollie Cornwell, who contributed much toward making me feel at home in Plains; to David Ewing and Linda Roberson of Carter Country Tours; to William and Mattie Beth Spires, the Reverend Bruce Edwards, Art Maggio, and Dr. John Robinson. And no one could visit Sumter County without owing a debt of gratitude to David and Faye West of Faye's Bar-B-Q Villa.

For
Miss Lillian,
without whom, this book—
and so much more—
could not have been.

Introduction

When I visited Plains, Georgia, in December of 1976, between the election and the inauguration, I was only one of many writers and photographers who swarmed over the town. I had come to write a book, but I stayed on to become a friend of Mrs. Lillian Carter and her family.

It's very easy to love Miss Lillian: she is forthright, honest about her feelings, high-spirited, and always unpredictable. It is more difficult to understand why she took a liking to me. It may have been because she is a born teacher, and she could see that I have much to learn. Whatever it was, our meeting was something of a miracle to me. It was my first day in Plains, and I was busily taking photographs of the people filing through the depot to speak to the mother of the newly elected President. "Hey," she called out (the Southern equivalent of *hello*), singling me out from the crowd. "Come over here and pull up a chair. Tell me what you're up to."

We exchanged bits of conversation between greetings to passers-by, amid the "hellos" and "God bless yous," punctuated by the pop of flashbulbs. And we continued our conversation later, over coffee in her home and over dinner at Faye's Bar-B-Q Villa.

Before dinner, we joined in a candlelight prayer vigil sponsored by the Quakers. It was held in front of her son's home and we left only when the Secret Service reminded us that the car was illegally parked.

In the wonder of discovering a new friend, I forgot about all the questions I was supposed to ask, such as "What was it like giving birth to a future president?" Instead we talked like old friends—about civil rights and peace and her experience in the Peace Corps in India—and enjoyed our similarity of interests.

Somewhere along the line, I forgot that I was talking to the mother of the thirty-ninth President because I became so fascinated with Miss Lillian, the unique human being. Amidst the noise and fun at Faye's, Miss Lillian communicated a special message to me: She revealed that she too had once been shy. And then she told me how to overcome my own shyness.

The experience may sound very simple in the telling; but it was not simple at all. There was something magical in it. There was the clear evidence of truth in her words and her manner. It is very easy to learn from this remarkable woman, and it is easy to see why she has produced remarkable children.

As our friendship grew, Miss Lillian began to refer to me as a member of the family. When she was ill in the hospital, and visitors were restricted, she would say, "Jim Neyland is a member of the family." No, I wasn't kinfolk, but I was becoming part of a wider family—those people who understand what she and her children are all about and who want to learn about the Carters.

Miss Lillian helped me to understand the special Carter qualities. I am indebted to her for the hours of reminiscence and conversation we shared. During that time, the picture of her famous son and her other remarkable children began to form vividly in my mind. I am most grateful for this firsthand glimpse into the First Family.

For that reason, this book is intended as a tribute to Miss Lillian. And, of course, to the children she has reared—not just Jimmy and Gloria and Ruth and Billy, but also Rosalynn and Sybil and all of the grandchildren.

It is also a tribute to all those in the "extended family of man" who have shown their faith in Jimmy Carter.

—*James Neyland*

The man from Plains in a solitary moment on St. Simon's Island, off the coast of Georgia. (UPI)

The Man from Plains

By day, the cars, vans, campers, and trailers create traffic such as this small town has never seen; at night, the procession thins to a trickle, but it never stops completely. They are not unlike participants in a religious pilgrimage, the people who stream steadily through Plains, Georgia.

They come from every state in the Union. Despite the curiosity and outward signs of tourism, they come in reverence and respect, wanting to see the new President's home, to speak to the people who know him well, perhaps to talk to a member of his family. They come hoping to find proof that what they have read and heard is true—that, at long last, they have managed to elect a man of their own, a man not unlike themselves, a president of the United States who will listen to the people, and who will act for them.

For most of the people of the United

States firmly believe their country still belongs to them. They want to have pride in, and hope for, their nation; they want to believe in the form of government that has been handed down to them with such care.

Despite corruption in high places; despite the shame of a war that lasted too long and perhaps never should have been; despite murders, rapes, muggings, and vice; despite the soaring divorce rate and despite scholarly predictions that their nation is on the decline—the people of the United States still believe in themselves. And they want to believe that the man from Plains, Georgia, is one of them. But they are cautious because they have been misled too many times by campaign rhetoric, and have later regretted their gullibility.

More than a generation has passed since a Missouri haberdasher brought the people of the United States out of a world war as the most powerful nation on earth. There has been little but trouble, despair, and disillusion ever since. That man from

The best chance of seeing Jimmy and Rosalynn is on Sunday morning at the Plains Baptist Church. (Wide World)

Missouri, by chance or by choice, was the last real man of the people the country saw in the presidency.

As the Bicentennial Year of 1976 approached, there seemed to be few reasons for hope and little cause for celebration. Even those usually most glib with patriotic rhetoric were cautious about celebrating an event that seemed more appropriately a wake than a time of rebirth. Inflation continued to spiral upward, and unemployment lines kept growing. The year 1976 was also an election year, and the people were being promised more of the same old philosophies that would keep the country going but not take it anywhere.

No elaborate Bicentennial expositions had been planned, no prideful displays of accomplishments at a World's Fair. Any celebrating to be done was being left to the people in the cities and towns around the country. Maybe that was what did it. In cities and towns everywhere, people of all ages, races, creeds, and colors joined together in celebration of themselves and of their differences and their unity. And maybe that's what made the people remember who they were and what power they could wield. It was a time of regeneration. And the biggest popular symbol of regeneration in 1976 proved to be Jimmy Carter.

Jimmy who?

James Earl Carter, Jr., of Plains, Georgia, was a man of relative obscurity in 1975. He had been Governor of the state of Georgia for a time, but now he was back to being an ordinary citizen—a farmer, a peanut farmer. And Jimmy Carter knew how the people felt, because he felt the same things himself.

When he announced that he was running for president, the newsmen called him "Jimmy Who." In the beginning, they said it in jest, in derision at the thought that an unknown, without long exposure by the press, could be elected to the highest office in the country.

But "Jimmy Who" took his case to the people. "Hello," he introduced himself on the streets of Iowa and New Hampshire, New York and Florida, "I'm Jimmy Carter, and I'm going to be your next President." And soon "Jimmy Who" became as proud a name as any other, because it represented the power of the ordinary man.

"Jimmy Who" did not claim to be a liberal, nor did he profess to be a conservative. Although the press and his opponents tried to pin him down, he avoided easy labels, because he knew that what the people wanted was neither liberal nor conservative, yet at the same time a little of both.

What was more important to Jimmy—and to the people—was the personal touch, a handshake, and his promise to do the best job possible. After all, those were the very same elements on which this country had been built—a handshake and a promise.

"Jimmy Who's" kind of politics kept the opposition laughing. They kept playing a new game: pin the issues on the peanut farmer. But with or without a blindfold, the people knew what the real issue was: honesty, and an earnest attempt to put the business of government back in order. The people had voted for issues before, and inevitably they had been let down. This time they were voting for hope, and for themselves.

Of course, there was the chance that they might be let down once again. This Jimmy Carter might not be all that he claimed to be. For all the average voter knew, the entire town of Plains, Georgia, might have been created by Hollywood or Madison Avenue. But Jimmy Carter *seemed* to be for real. There was that family of his. Even the most fertile imaginations could not have created that family. They were everywhere at once—Rosalynn, and Miss Lillian, Amy, Billy, Gloria, and Ruth. They were all so different. And when they talked about the issues, they didn't always agree with each other. Hollywood would have made them more consistent,

The people of Plains, Jimmy Carter's friends and neighbors, those who know him best, have been his most ardent supporters. Gathered in front of the Carter Warehouse to watch the Democratic convention, they waved and cheered when his name was placed in nomination. (Wide World)

and Madison Avenue just never could have created a mother who was a Peace Corps veteran, one sister who was a motorcycle nut, another who was an evangelist, and a brother who was the beer-drinking owner of a service station. A family like that just had to be real.

So the people allowed themselves to believe—not wildly or passionately, but with a quiet faith and hope. They went to the polls and they voted, maybe with a little prayer just before they pulled the lever or marked the ballot, "Please God, let it be right this time."

With this insecure faith, the people of the United States voted the man from Plains into the office of President of the United States. The man just had something about him that made you believe.

It is this same something that brings the people to Plains, Georgia, in unbelievable numbers. Some come to substantiate their faith, and some come to express their faith. "We're behind him," they will say to Miss Lillian, patting her on the back or shaking her hand. "We believe he's going to do a good job." All of them are expressing something they have not expressed in a long, long time—a sense of national pride, pride that they are part of a nation of people, as diverse as any in history, yet able to join together to defeat those who would seek to subjugate them.

The Americans who come to Plains to honor Jimmy Carter are of all religious faiths and some are even devout atheists. They are young and old, bearded and clean-shaven, long-haired and neatly coiffed. The come in families and singly, black, white, yellow, and brown.

Now the people come to Jimmy, driving into Plains hoping to see the man they have elected. First stop for the visitors is the Plains railroad depot, which served as the presidential campaign headquarters— "where it all began."
(Neyland)

To the right of Highway 280, across the fields, are the Plains High School and the Plains Baptist Church.
(Neyland)

Jimmy took his campaign to the people, approaching them on the street with hand outstretched, saying, "Hello, I'm Jimmy Carter, and I'm going to be your next president." (Wide World)

Diverse elements of the contemporary American South, represented on the platform of the Plains railroad depot: a dog sleeping in the shade, a Coca-Cola machine, a lectern, and a portrait of "Jimmy Who." (Neyland)

It has become an unusual event for Rosalynn, Jimmy, or Amy to walk freely about Plains unattended by Secret Service agents. A rare moment after the Democratic convention was the opening of the Back Porch Café on Main Street, when the two most recognizable Carter women—Miss Lillian and Rosalynn—enjoyed sandwiches and soft drinks together. (Wide World)

They are respectful toward the town they visit, understanding that they are guests and that their presence is altering the natural order of the small town. "I grew up in a town like this," they say nostalgically, or "I used to visit my grandmother, and she lived in a town like this." They tread carefully. They don't want Plains to become a standard tourist trap.

They talk to the townspeople and are amazed at how friendly and open the people of Plains are. They are just like the folks back home—or like the folks back home used to be. Maybe the visitors will buy an antique cabinet from Jimmy's cousin, Mr. Hugh Carter, or sit and talk to Mr. Hugh's father, Mr. Alton. Yes, they know people back home like Mr. Hugh and Mr. Alton.

Perhaps the visitors will run into Miss Allie Smith, Rosalynn's mother, doing her grocery shopping or sitting behind the reception desk at the train depot. So quiet is Miss Allie and so ladylike, that the visitors may overlook her at first, unless they are taken with something familiar about her face. Or unless they happen to have a baby with them, in which case Miss Allie's natural reserve completely disappears. And when Miss Allie's face breaks into a wide, loving grin, so much like Rosalynn's, the visitors can't mistake her.

But the one person everybody recognizes instantly is Miss Lillian. Now *that*, they say to themselves, is a mother unlike any other mother. But when they say it, they say it with respect and with love. Because Lillian Carter is an American original. She is a single small amalgam of all the qualities that have made the American character great: toughness welded with an unbounded concern for others and a preference for the underdog; honesty to the

point of bluntness; a distaste for sentiment; and a resolve not to grow old in her heart and mind despite the passing years.

Until the strain took a toll on her health, Miss Lillian would sit in the train depot each afternoon greeting the visitors, shaking hands, signing autographs, and accepting the good wishes and the expressions of faith from the people. Those visitors who passed through Plains before the doctor ordered Miss Lillian to slow down had the opportunity to see their faith affirmed and reinforced. Yes, Miss Lillian was real, a bit feisty and a bit cranky at times, but the kind of mother who couldn't possibly raise a liar and a cheat.

The train depot—the presidential campaign headquarters where it all began—is the first attraction for those who come to Plains. But across the tracks, just a few feet off U.S. Highway 280, is a shrine of equal importance, a most improbable shrine— Billy Carter's Amoco station. Just about everybody who comes through town manages to find the need to buy some gas at Billy's station, and some of them time their empty tanks to a moment when the President's younger brother is there.

Of all the Carter children, Billy is probably the one most like Miss Lillian. Outspoken, genial, down-to-earth, he is the favorite of the family and of the people. Oh, the people know all about Billy's beer drinking, and about his clowning around with all the boys who hang out at the station; but even the strictest moralists don't disapprove. Compared to the kind of public vices the people have seen in recent years, drinking beer is a virtue. After all, everybody likes to have a little harmless fun now and then. In fact, just about everybody can identify with Billy Carter; he is generous to a fault, he is outgoing and friendly, and he doesn't take himself too seriously. If there are any qualities that are truly American, those are they.

But Billy Carter is a bit more than just a "good ol' boy." His eyes are like Jimmy's eyes, holding that special intelligence that

7

At Jimmy's request, his mother, known to all as Miss Lillian, greeted visitors to Plains daily for six weeks after the election. After several weeks of Miss Lillian's shaking hands and signing autographs, her doctor put her arm in a sling and admonished her not to use it. (Neyland)

seems to distinguish all the Carters—Miss Lillian, Gloria, Ruth, Billy, Amy, Rosalynn, and Jimmy. It is the factor that distinguishes the Carters from the family next door. Those eyes seem to take in everything at a glance, to perceive and understand and know a situation, or a person, intuitively. They are not harsh or judging eyes; they are sympathetic, concerned, caring.

If a visitor is lucky enough to meet Rosalynn Carter, what is first evident—aside from that special quality of intelligence—is that she is quiet, possibly just a little bit shy. When she finds it necessary to step out of her role of wife and mother to be a public figure, she seems to do it with effort. She does not do it coldly or condescendingly, or with any signs of regret, for she remains the same, genuine, caring woman she is in private with only her family around her; but she does it with the manner of a quiet-natured woman who has found it necessary to come out of her shell.

What is most amazing about Rosalynn is that, with all the campaigning she has done, after all the thousands of different people she has met, she has not developed that hard veneer so many political wives wrap around themselves. She continues to greet each person she meets as an individual, distinct and different from all the rest. At times, the strain and fatigue show in little lines around her bright, pretty eyes, but she never grows unkind. Her manner suggests that she is a woman with that Southern heritage of good breeding, and with all the domestic virtues, but with the fortitude to meet any demand willingly and with grace.

The greatest privilege of all for the visitor to Plains is to meet the man himself—the President. He seems to be what the people prayed that he would be—he is a *good* man. He is also, at the very least, a charitable man.

Perhaps too much has already been said, in too glib a manner, about Jimmy Carter's religious beliefs. He would be one of the first to agree with that, considering his religious beliefs to be a matter of concern only between him and God. But they are important in measuring the man. His Christian faith is probably the one most important factor in understanding the man Jimmy Carter. It is the one factor that most perplexes and confuses writers and newsmen who try to probe his motives and to explain him: he is simply *too* good to be true. It is not that he is a goody-goody, sanctimonious sort of Christian. It's just that he doesn't seem to have to try to recall the Golden Rule; it simply comes naturally to him. Anyone meeting him or talking with him automatically has his undivided attention. He is concerned about his neighbor, and he really seems to love his neighbor just as he loves himself.

This is not meant to suggest that Jimmy Carter is some kind of a saint. "Oh, Jimmy has his faults," Miss Lillian is quick to point out. But, when pressed to name some, Miss Lillian has to think hard. Her brow furrows, and her lips purse slightly with a vague sort of frustration. "Well," she laughs finally, "I guess his biggest fault is that he doesn't have enough faults." And then she adds seriously, "One fault is that he expects too much of other people, and he's sometimes impatient with them. But he doesn't expect any more of others than he expects of himself." She pauses, and then adds, "*And* he has a temper." But Jimmy Carter's impatience and temperament show up very rarely, and only in very serious matters.

Despite his highly religious nature, he remains a man of the people. He enjoys relaxing with family and friends. He likes to have quiet moments to hike through the fields alone or with Rosalynn or one of the children. Regrettably, with the constant attention of newsmen and the Secret Service, those moments are growing more and more rare.

Jimmy is very much aware of the problem involved in removing the president from the people, and he is aware that it is not so much a problem for the people as it is for the president. Too many presidents in recent years have become enamored of the trappings of state, forgetting their humble origins.

Jimmy Carter is determined to live no differently in the White House from the way he lives in Plains, Georgia. This is perhaps as much to remind himself of who he is as to remind others of what country this is.

Sure, grits are being served in the White House. Why not? They're good, they're nourishing, they're eaten by lots of good honest people in our country. If grits are what a boy grew up with, and if he likes

them, why shouldn't he eat them, even in Washington? And why shouldn't he wear jeans? A man can't live in a suit and tie twenty-four hours a day just because he happens to be head of state. It's the man that makes the difference, not the suit.

Jimmy Carter is a plain man. He intends to remain so. He does not feel that he or his country have to prove to anyone that they have taste and culture. He knows that taste and culture are not acquired and im-

At home in Plains during the campaign, Jimmy, Rosalynn, and Amy appeared at a rally on Main Street. Despite the public eye, Amy removed her shoe and sock to scratch where it itched. (Wide World)

ported, but indigenous to the people. After two hundred years, America has a heritage; and a culture. It is what it is; it is its people. That is the unspoken message of Jimmy Carter—the message he conveys in his life rather than with his words.

If the visitors to Plains are fortunate enough to meet the man, this is the man they will see—unpretentious, perhaps even humble; a man, not unlike them-

Jimmy's cousin, Hugh Carter, sells antiques in Plains, but he also sells worms all over the world. The headquarters for the world's largest worm farm is on the main street of Plains, next door to the Carter press office. (Wide World)

Billy Carter's appearance is deceiving. He looks like your average beer-drinking "good ol' boy," but he is also a capable businessman and a loving husband and father. (Neyland)

selves, but somehow a very special plain man.

It is impossible to say precisely what it is that has made Jimmy Carter special. His unique quality is a combination of so many different things. His is a very ordinary family, but also possibly just a bit extraordinary in its ability to accept and love each of its members as a distinct individual. It is his religious faith, a common and simple religion, that is uncommon because it is as much practiced as preached. It is his rural Southern heritage, which has emphasized hard work, and a closeness to nature and the soil and a common caring for one's neighbors, that is a special heritage because it harbors the thoughts and principles of leaders like Thomas Jefferson and Andrew Jackson.

Entering Plains on U.S. Highway 280, the visitor first sees the industrial section of town, and the new water tower with the Stars and Stripes painted brightly at the top. Beneath the tower are the mobile homes that house NBC, CBS, and ABC. Straight ahead is the business district. (Neyland)

Jimmy Carter is also a man of the twentieth century. He is the first president to be born in a hospital. He has grown up with radio and television and motion pictures. He enjoys rock music and baseball and auto racing. And he was educated as an engineer, that most pragmatic of twentieth century occupations.

This is the story of Jimmy Carter, the man, the husband, the father, the son and the farmer; the dreamer and the doer. It is also the story of the Carter family—an extraordinary ordinary family that produced a President of the people—a family with an integrity and compassion that it passed on to all its children and to Jimmy Carter in full measure.

It is also the story of Rosalynn Carter, a generous wife and mother, a dedicated supporter, yet a woman in her own right, with the same Carter compassion and integrity. And it is the story of her family and its roots in America's South.

Miss Allie Smith, Rosalynn's mother, can usually go about her business in Plains without being noticed by the many visitors. Even when she visits with the people in the railroad depot, she remains quiet and reserved—except with small children. (Neyland)

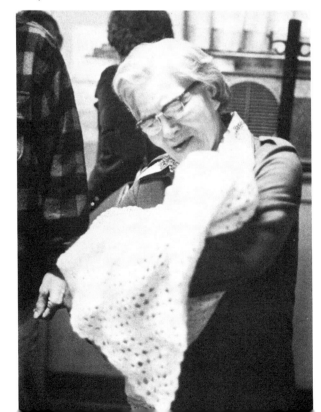

This is not a book about politics or campaigning or smoke-filled back rooms. It is not about the men in high places who shun the people, or about smear headlines and secret treaties. It is a warm and intimate sojourn with Jimmy Carter and the Carter family—a family embodying all the best qualities of American culture and the Southern heritage.

To understand this man and this family, this story must begin in the past—with a visit to an earlier Plains.

As the campaign wore on, so did the Democratic candidate's shoes. He spent much of his time on his feet on the streets, meeting the voters. (Wide World)

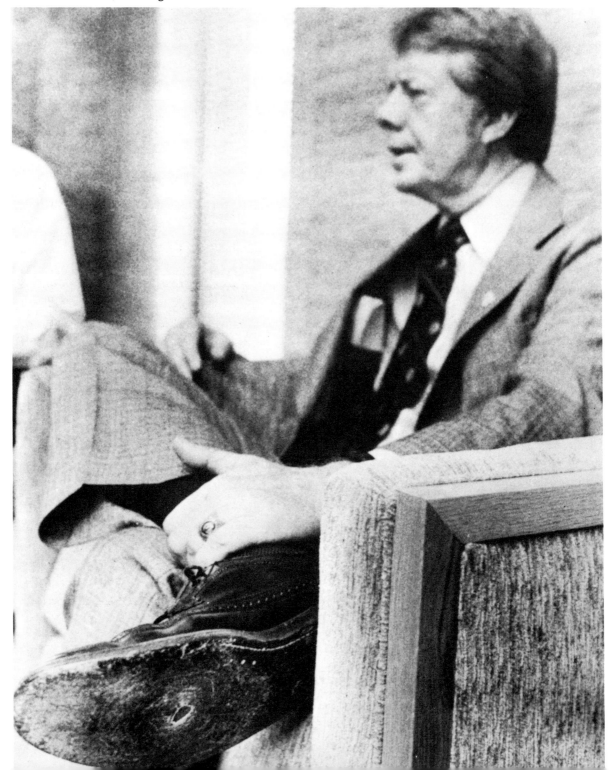

Roots in Red Clay

James Earl Carter, Jr., was very prompt for his first appointment, on October 1, 1924. "They clocked him," Miss Lillian recalls with a mischievous air that is meant to mask the natural pride. "Jimmy was born on the dot at 7 A.M. He was very punctual from the very beginning. He just couldn't stand to be late."

Jimmy's birthplace is now a convalescent home, but, when Jimmy was born, and when Miss Lillian worked there as a nurse, it was the Wise Hospital, founded and run by the three Doctors Wise—or the three Wise men, as some prefer to call them. The hospital is a long, one-story, white structure, not unlike other medical buildings around the country.

What is unusual about the Wise Hospital is that it existed in a town the size of Plains. But in the twenties, Plains was considered a boom town. Its population had risen to six hundred, and the freight trains that loaded up in Plains were taking away the largest shipments of hogs and cattle in the country. In 1920, the Wise Brothers—Thad, Sam, and Bowman—built their hospital. Three years later, students moved into the town's splendid new high school, with facilities for three hundred students. The town even boasted a hotel, which stood on the site of what is now Billy Carter's service station.

These changes brought education and a positive spirit of progress to Plains, but the principal livelihood continued to be farming. The rich red clay was ideal for growing staples such as cotton, watermelon, corn, and peanuts. That rich red soil and the mild weather had been the main attraction of Sumter County ever since the 1830s, when the first settlers had moved in and the Creek Indians were moved out.

The first Carter moved to Sumter County in 1851, but he was not the first Carter in America, nor even the first in Georgia. But all of them, in the Southern agrarian tradition, were planters and farmers—starting with Thomas Carter, who migrated from England to Virginia in 1637—on down for eleven generations, as they slowly moved south and west with the opening up of new frontiers.

It was the fifth generation, in the person of Kindred Carter, who migrated from North Carolina to Richmond County, Georgia, late in the eighteenth century. And it was Kindred's grandson, Wiley Carter, who almost a hundred years later, made the move southward to Sumter County.

The early Carters were typical of the first English settlers. To them, the owning of land was an essential of life; the relationship between man and soil was a deeply personal one. It was the land that made them independent; it was the land that gave them dignity. Their English heritage and the isolation of the frontier both contributed toward making them a very self-sufficient people, growing or manufacturing all the basic necessities on their own property. They grew or raised all their own food, and put it up or cured it for use during the winters. They made their own clothing, using skins, hides, or homespun, purchasing finer cloth only for special wear. There was generally a blacksmith shop on the property for making or repairing their tools and implements.

To do all this required manpower, and the Southern farmer and planter had three ways of remaining independent: one way, in the early days, was to buy slaves; another way was to permit other settlers, with less ability or less luck than the landholders, to sharecrop part of the land; the most important way was to have big families—the bigger the better. With big families, however, the younger sons often found it necessary to move on with the frontier. That is how Jimmy Carter comes to have so many cousins, twice, thrice, and

Genealogical chart of the Carters, Gordys, Smiths, and Murrays—ancestors of Jimmy and Rosalynn Carter. (Neyland)

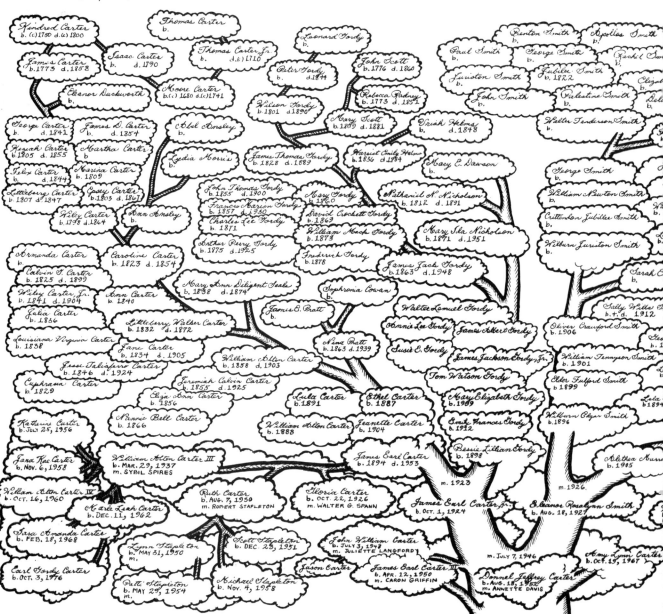

The Plains Convalescent Home today. Fifty-two years ago, it was the Wise Hospital, and there James Earl Carter, Jr. was born. The small window of the room where he was delivered is seen between the columns, to the left of the door. (Neyland)

Miss Lillian says that Jimmy Carter was "ordinary." What she means, in Yankee language, is that he was a typical Southern boy. Jeans were his standard dress, and he spent his summers barebacked and barefooted, roaming about the fields and woods. (Neyland, courtesy of the Carter family)

The gravestone of Wiley Carter in the Carter family cemetery. His home, known as the Battle Place, still stands. Wiley was the grandson of Kindred Carter, the first member of the family to settle in Georgia, and the seventh generation in America. (Neyland)

four times removed, all over the United States.

Because the community of a single farm or plantation could number upward of thirty (sometimes numbering beyond one hundred), laws, rules, and codes of behavior were needed, and there had to be a single authority; herein lie the origins of Southern Baptist religion. Trying to determine which came first in the Southern heritage—the belief in God, or the need for God—is like debating chickens and eggs. Suffice it to say that the Baptist religion functioned very well, and the patriarch of the family was almost always a deeply religious man, and a very strict disciplinarian.

It was into this heritage that James Earl Carter, Jr., came. Jimmy was the first child born to Earl and Lillian Carter, and even though he was thin and somewhat small, he was a healthy baby. He was not a particularly precocious child, though he did start walking at ten months. But, knowing Jimmy's concern for punctuality, maybe he thought it was time to get moving about on his own.

Mr. Earl and Miss Lillian had been married only a little over a year when Jimmy arrived on the scene, and it can be said that he was, at least in one way, a "planned" baby—planned by Miss Lillian, though not quite as early as she would have liked.

"Earl and I were engaged to be married when I was still in nurse's training," Miss Lillian remembers. "I wanted to forget about nursing entirely, and just get married. But Earl insisted that I finish. So I went to Atlanta for six months, finished my training, came home, and we were married three months later. After we were married, I kept on working at the hospital in Plains. But I was tired of nursing; it's a hard job. I wanted to get pregnant first thing so I wouldn't have to work anymore."

While reflecting on this, Miss Lillian's face suggests she is not entirely serious— that she's kidding just a little bit. She's kidding when she implies that she didn't like

Earl Carter, Jimmy's father, in his World War I uniform. (Neyland, courtesy of the Carter family)

nursing, that maybe she was too lazy for such a demanding pursuit. When one gets to know her well, it becomes obvious that she could never have the slightest inclination toward laziness, and that she became a nurse because of a deeply rooted compassion for others.

But what her story reveals of Mr. Earl's character is very probably true. From all accounts, he seems to have been a practical, serious-minded man, just the kind who would have insisted that his wife have a training on which she could rely, if it became necessary. Certainly, in those early years of their marriage, there was no certainty of financial security. Earl could provide very well for their immediate needs, but the sort of life he wanted for his family would be a few years in the making; and he knew how uncertain life could be.

Earl Carter had been only seven at the

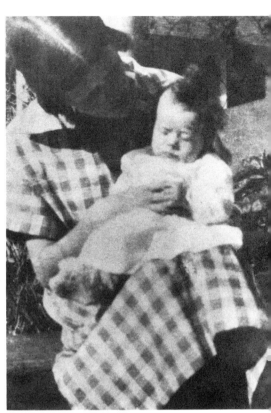

There are few photographs of Miss Lillian in earlier years. More often than not, she was behind the camera taking pictures of her children. Right: Miss Lillian Carter holding her infant son Jimmy in her lap. (Neyland, courtesy of the Carter family)

---

untimely death of his father, William Carter, who had been shot in a dispute over the ownership of a desk. At the time, Earl's mother, Nina Pratt Carter, was expecting William's fifth child; and, although the family moved into the town of Plains so that sons Alton and Earl could get jobs to help out, Earl knew it was still a difficult life without a father. If anything should ever happen to him, Earl had the comfort of knowing Lillian would be able to take care of herself and the children. His wife's nursing training was a safeguard.

As things turned out, however, through initiative and hard work, Earl had his finances in good shape in only a few years. Soon after he and Lillian were married, Earl bought the only thing he ever bought on credit—seven hundred acres of good farm land—and he paid it off as rapidly as he could. Meanwhile, he and his wife lived in

Jimmy at age one. An unusual photo because he's wearing shoes and he's sitting still. (Neyland, courtesy of the Carter family)

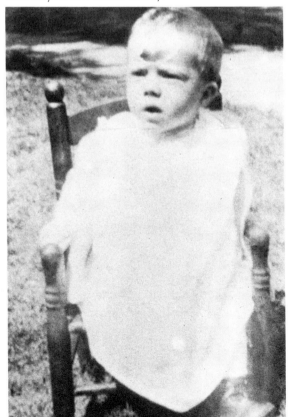

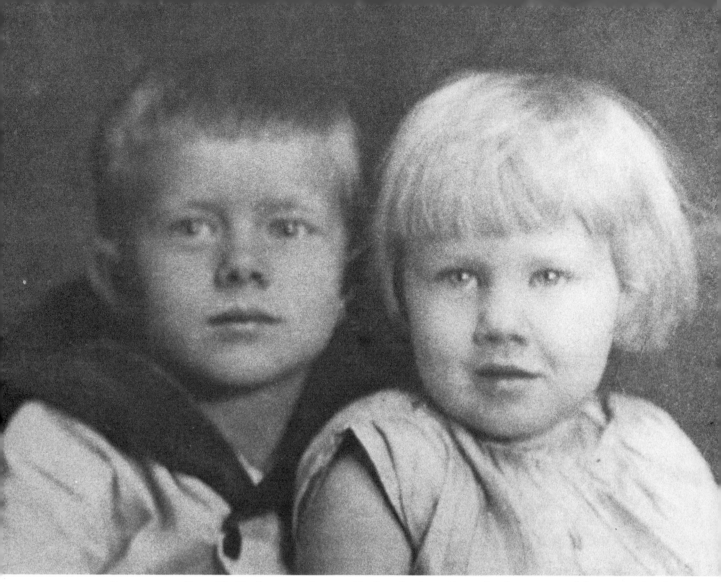

Jimmy at age five with Gloria at age three—"Hot" and "Gogo." (Neyland, courtesy of the Carter family)

The house at Archery as seen from the railroad tracks. The railroad right of way formed a shortcut to town, passing right by his grandmother Nina's house on the way to the depot. The grove of trees in the distance is the pecan grove that Jimmy, as a small child, helped his father to plant. (Neyland)

Looking along the railroad tracks in Plains toward Archery. Jimmy's grandmother's house is off the tracks to the right, about a block beyond the depot. (Neyland)

Mr. Earl Carter late in life looked more like the successful businessman than the struggling farmer. Jimmy recalls a rare occasion when his father was fitted for a suit; when the suit arrived much too large, no one in the family dared to laugh. (Neyland, courtesy of the Carter family)

A view of Plains, looking from the business district across the park toward the intersection of Highway 280 (Church Street) and Hudson Street. The two-story house on the corner, in the right of the picture, is the house where Mr. Earl and Miss Lillian lived before Jimmy was born. Their small apartment was on the second floor. (Neyland)

Jimmy's parade—riding Lady, with Lady Lee, and his dog following. They are headed in the direction of the woodpile, an important part of any home heated by fireplaces. (Neyland, courtesy of the Carter family)

moved again. By the time Gloria, the second child, came along, the Carters lived in a house owned by Alton Carter that had four rooms and—a new luxury for the family—a bathroom. But they would soon have to give up that luxury when Earl Carter provided his family with a home of their own. That change may have been what caused Jimmy mistakenly to look upon his childhood as one of poverty.

The new home that Earl Carter bought for his family was at the little settlement of Archery, not far outside Plains. The facilities may have been a bit crude by modern standards, but they were certainly far removed from poverty (the house actually had its own tennis court). When asked about the description Jimmy has given of his childhood, Miss Lillian shows traces of exasperation. It's a question she has obviously grown tired of answering.

"Jimmy writes in his book about how poor we were; we weren't poor; we just didn't have the modern conveniences. We didn't have an indoor toilet; we didn't have electric lights; we didn't have running water. We had a pump on the back

Jimmy at the fence, feeding Lady Lee. (Neyland, courtesy of the Carter family)

various apartments in Plains, moving from one to another as better ones became available and affordable. The claim to be the first residence of Jimmy Carter is made for a number of houses in Plains, including a very beautiful Victorian structure right in the heart of town, now owned by Art Maggio, who runs the Plains Coin Shop. In fact, the Maggio house almost became Jimmy Carter's first home, but the stairs were a problem. The Carters had a small apartment—one room, a hall, and a kitchen—upstairs in that house. "But I was so pregnant," Miss Lillian recalls, "I couldn't get up and down the stairs, so we had to move to a house down the street."

That house, the true first home of Jimmy, burned down, and the family porch, but we lived just as well as anybody else who lived in the country before rural electrification.

"It was a nice house. It had six rooms. There were fireplaces in four of them, and we burned logs. In the kitchen, we had a wood stove, just like everybody else had. As soon as it was possible to have modern conveniences out in the country, Earl had them put in, but they just weren't available when Jimmy was little."

The Carters moved into their new home just before Jimmy's third birthday. The day of the move was an important occasion, and the entire family— Earl, Lillian, Jimmy, and Gloria—went out to the house early in the morning. However, in the excitement, Earl had forgotten to bring the keys to the house. With the family's elation quickly fading into frustration, Earl came up with the solution. He helped his son to climb into the house through a window, and Jimmy then went to the front door and unbolted it to let the family in. It was an adventurous beginning for young Jimmy's rural life. The day-to-day life might have seemed plain or crude or hard, but it was the kind of existence that many people long to return to today.

There were trees for climbing, and woods and swamps and creeks for hunting and fishing. There were the railroad tracks that ran parallel to the road that fronted the house; a child could time his day and his play by the sound of the train whistles; and the railroad right of way provided pebbles just the right size for a slingshot. An old Indian lived in a house just down the road, and he could tell stories that would make Jimmy's blood curdle.

There were nuts and fruits and berries that could be picked and eaten right off the tree or vine. And there were the magic and fascination of the seasons. Fruits and vegetables were canned. Hogs were slaughtered and cured, with the parts that couldn't be cured being pickled and canned for souse (usually pickled hog's brains). At the commissary, a big barnlike

structure, the canned and cured provisions were sold to the hired hands and share-croppers, and each of the children occasionally put in time behind the counter.

When Jimmy was seven, he was given a beautiful pony named Lady. Lady was a birthday gift from his father, bought the day before from a man in De Soto, Georgia, and hauled to Plains in time to surprise

Jimmy, in his early teens, with his favorite pet, **Bozo.** (Neyland, courtesy of the Carter family)

Jimmy at his party. For a long time, the boy and the pony were inseparable; Jimmy would dash out the back door shouting, "Lady!" The pony would come running and off they would ride.

When Lady gave birth to a colt, Lady Lee, the rides sometimes had the appearance of a parade—first Jimmy and Lady, then Lady Lee, and finally the bird dog, Nig. Later,

Annie Mae Hollis looked after the Carter children and their chums as well. Here, Annie Mae holds Ruth Carter in her lap, while Gloria Carter sits beside her. Standing, crouched behind, are Jimmy Carter, Fred Foster, and Rembert Forrest. (Neyland, courtesy of the Carter family)

there was another dog—Jimmy's favorite —a bulldog named Bozo. But Bozo met the fate of many country dogs. He was an excellent hunting dog, and Jimmy lent him to a friend for a hunting trip, during which Bozo was hit by a car and killed.

Animals were not Jimmy's only playmates. He had friends all over the place, not to mention his sisters, and he was far from being a lonely country child. One friend of Jimmy's was Rembert Forrest, who lived about five miles away; when they visited with one another it was for a week or two at a time. Another friend was Fred Foster, who lived nearby for a time. But Jimmy's

best friends came from the black community, because they did not move in and out of the area so rapidly. The best of all those best friends was A. D. Davis. Jimmy and A. D. did everything there was to do together. They rode the mules, they rode Lady, they went fishing, and they sold peanuts. As Jimmy remembers it, pulling, cleaning, and boiling peanuts was hard work, and selling them was lonely. But his sister Gloria and Miss Lillian remember it differently.

"That was a project they all did together—Jimmy and A. D. and Gloria— even Ruth. Gloria and Ruth get mad when

Jimmy says that he did that all by himself. They would pull the peanuts and wash them, and I would boil them. We had a little basket, and we'd put ten or fifteen little sacks of peanuts in the basket, and Jimmy and A. D. would sell them for a nickel a sack in the town. Sometimes they would ride downtown in the car with Jimmy's father, and sometimes they would walk down the road to town."

Gloria's memory is even more specific. "Jimmy didn't clean those peanuts; I did! He paid me a nickel a day to do it for him. Then he told me that if I buried my nickels in a specific place, they would grow into a money tree. I planted my nickels; and when nothing grew, I tried to dig them up, but they were gone."

The disappearance of the nickels was just one of the many woes of being Jimmy Carter's little sister. He teased both sisters mercilessly. The majority of the six peach-tree switchings Jimmy received as a child came as a result of tricks he played on Gloria and Ruth. Jimmy himself has written about one of those switchings. For some unexplained reason, Gloria threw a monkey wrench at Jimmy, and he retaliated by shooting her in the rear with his BB gun. For several hours, Gloria listened for the sound of Earl's car on the road, bursting into tears every time she thought she heard him approaching. When he did finally arrive, Gloria told her story tearfully, and Jimmy got his punishment. Ruth was also the butt of Jimmy's mischief, and the reason for some of his punishment. Miss Lillian recalls another of his switchings.

"Do you know what pepper sauce is? We used to make a lot of pepper sauce out at the commissary. We would use some of it and sell some to the hands. Once, Jimmy picked up one of the peppers and told Ruth to taste it because it was real sweet. She bit down on it, and it nearly burned her up. He got a whipping for that."

However, Jimmy was more mischievous than mean. There was never any real hostility or enmity between him and his sisters.

Jimmy posing formally in front of the house at Archery with one of the many family dogs. It must have been a special occasion, since he wears not only a shirt and shoes but also a tie. (Neyland, courtesy of the Carter family)

Between pranks, Jimmy loved and looked after his younger siblings. A very special bond of affection grew up among the children, and it persists today, extending to the husbands and wives, the nieces and nephews.

Jimmy was two when his first sister arrived on the scene. He wasn't quite able to pronounce her name properly, though, and "Gloria" came out as "Gogo." The rest of the family picked up the affectionate form, and it stuck. Gogo had the plump beauty of a cherub, but she could be as impish and fun-loving as her older brother. To the outsider today, Gloria seems to be the sibling most like Jimmy. She has the same blend of contradictions: she's quiet and perceptively reflective as well as outgoing with down-home good spirits. Gloria is also the most private member of the family, trying as much as possible to live as she and her husband Walter lived before the limelight hit them. "I'm jes' folks," she tells anyone who questions her. "You wouldn't be interested in me."

Some of Jimmy Carter's qualities can be seen in the other children as well. Ruth, nicknamed Boopydoop by Mr. Earl, shows evidence of the tremendous drive and energy that lie hidden beneath Jimmy's quiet surface. She has the same compassion and concern for others that the entire family shares, but it comes out with such urgency and so strong a dedication in her, that some call her a preacher, an evangelist, or a faith healer, though she considers herself merely a lecturer.

For seven years, Ruth was the baby in the family; then along came Billy. With such a wide span of ages (Jimmy was twelve at the time), Billy became the baby brother the family loved and doted upon, almost as if he had five parents instead of the usual two. But Billy wasn't spoiled, even if he did receive so much attention. The same strict code of right and wrong, the same discipline, applied to him as it did to the others.

Billy today is a fun-loving "good ol' boy," and that side of him has been given so much coverage in the press that he seems to be a caricature. But there is another side to Billy Carter that is rarely seen: that of the family man and the successful businessman. He is dedicated as much to hard work, and to a concern for others, as he is to having fun. And his deep love for his children has brought its own rewards. In a time when children are notorious for being spoiled, confused, and uncontrollable, the children of Billy and Sybil Carter are respectful and considerate, as well as fun-loving.

That special combination of love and discipline was the contribution of Mr. Earl Carter, although, because of Miss Lillian's strong personality, most people today assume that she was the dominant parent. Her strength has always been a personal strength, and her method of influencing her children has been by her example, by the way she has lived her life.

Miss Lillian was devoted to her husband, and she still is, even though he died almost twenty-five years ago. "I'm a one-man woman," she explains, her suddenly misty eyes accenting the fact that she still misses Mr. Earl. "I've never even looked at another man, and I don't believe that Earl was ever untrue to me, even though he was the kind of man who would certainly have had the opportunity."

The relationship of absolute faithfulness was only one of the examples the elder Carters set for their children. While the children were growing up, Miss Lillian continued to take on nursing assignments, more out of her desire to care for others than out of any need to add income. She was a true example of Christian charity.

She also set an example, either intentionally or unintentionally, by her great appetite for reading. Plains had no library, and books had to be purchased either from a bookstore in Columbus or through a mail-order book club, but she managed to read four or five books a week. Mr. Earl liked to read, too, but his eyesight was so bad that he could only read the papers

It's difficult to look into a camera and say "Peanuts" with a blinding sun directly behind the photographer. Standing in the doorway is Mr. Earl Carter. In front of him are the three older children: **Gloria, Ruth, and Jimmy.** (Neyland, courtesy of the Carter family)

himself, and those only in the daylight and with his very thick glasses. At night, Miss Lillian often read to him. But she and the children read avidly for their own pleasure at any opportunity. Their best time for reading was at the breakfast table, after Mr. Earl had left for work. They would sit together and read for thirty or forty minutes, until the school bus came.

"Many people think this habit was so funny," Miss Lillian chortles. "But it wasn't funny to us; it was standard procedure. I

James Jackson Gordy, known as Jim Jack, was Miss Lillian's father. The family's interest in politics had its origin in Jim Jack Gordy, a district campaign manager for Congressman Tom Watson and the postmaster in Richland, Georgia. His most noteworthy accomplishment was the concept of Rural Free Delivery; he gave the idea to Tom Watson, who put it through Congress. Right: **Mary Ida Nicholson Gordy, from Chattahoochee County, Georgia. Jim Jack and Mary Ida were married in 1888 and had nine children, the fourth being Bessie Lillian Gordy, "Miss Lillian."** (Neyland, courtesy of the Carter family)

remember the first set of books Jimmy read—the first set I gave him. They were the Tarzan books. That was kind of heavy reading for him then. He went through all the Hardy Boys books, all the little boy books, and then he went on to adult books. All my children read just as much; but I think there was that one difference in Jimmy—he read the adult books when he was much younger. He read anything he wanted to in my house. I never have censored a book. But, of course, we never had any pornography in those days."

Perhaps the best example that Miss Lillian set for her children was one of complete frankness and honesty, her unequivocating manner of being precisely who and what she was. That was the trait the Carter children inherited from the Gordy side of the family, or perhaps more specifically from Miss Lillian and her father, Jim Jack Gordy, who had been postmaster at Richland, Georgia, and who

had been active in state politics. Like the Carters, the Gordys were Baptists, and their religion was a very active one; it was a part of one's daily life—doing things for others, visiting the lonely, caring for the sick, aiding the needy, and helping out those who were in trouble.

There were other influences on the children, as well. Prominent among these was that of Grandmother Nina, Earl's mother, who lived by herself in Plains. Each of the grandchildren had a night of the week to stay over with Miss Nina to keep her company. Jimmy recalls that his night was Friday. But on school days, the children also had their lunches at Miss Nina's, since it was too far to go home for lunch. They paid Miss Nina a nickel apiece for their sandwiches.

There were teachers, too, who influenced the children's development. Miss Julia Coleman and Mr. Young Thompson Sheffield had perhaps the greatest impact.

Miss Julia was crippled, and almost blind, but she was a fine English teacher. It was she who persuaded Jimmy to read *War and Peace* when he was twelve, and it was she who guided his reading from that time on. But she was interested in conveying more than just a love of good literature; she also gave her students an understanding and appreciation of music, art and the theater.

During the years that Jimmy was in school, Miss Julia was the superintendent, and Mr. Y. T. Sheffield was the principal, as well as the school coach. Together, they formed a team that endeavored to mold educated minds and healthy bodies.

However, in a rural school system thirty to forty years ago, that could be a difficult task. One of Jimmy's former schoolmates recalls, "Several of us boys were really too old to be going to school; by the time we got out, we were grown men, what with being left back for various reasons. And I guess we were pretty rough, always getting into trouble. Jimmy was smaller than we were, and younger. Whenever we went in

Miss Julia Coleman, English teacher and school superintendent, and Mr. Young Thomas Sheffield, principal and school coach—the two major influences on Jimmy Carter's education. Miss Julia, crippled and nearly blind in her later years, was the teacher Jimmy mentioned in his inaugural address. (Neyland, courtesy of the Carter family)

Grandmother Nina Carter's house in Plains today. It was here that Jimmy spent his Friday nights, keeping his grandmother company. (Neyland)

A school portrait of Jimmy at about age seventeen.
(Neyland, courtesy of the Carter family)

for any kind of mischief, Jimmy wouldn't go along."

Miss Lillian confirms that Jimmy was very serious about school and his studies. "The only time he ever had any trouble with a teacher, it wasn't Jimmy's fault; it was mine. It was once when he got a B in spelling and Jimmy was very good at spelling, and as far as I know he never missed a word. At the time he was striving so hard to get good grades so he could get into Annapolis, one of his teachers gave him a B-plus in spelling instead of an A. I called up Miss Julia Coleman, and I said, 'Miss Julia, Jimmy's teacher has given him a B-plus instead of an A, saying that he misspelled one word. I want you just to investigate it to be sure. So far as I know, he's never misspelled one.' "

During high school, Jimmy set his sights on a military career, and he was determined to go to Annapolis. His uncle, Tom

Gordy, was in military life, and Jimmy idolized him. In the early years of World War II, the family received word that Tom had been killed, and the news must have had a profound effect on young Jimmy. At the close of the war, however, they were overjoyed to learn that Tom had not been killed but had been captured by the Japanese and held in a prison camp.

Another strong influence on the Carter children, and perhaps on the whole family, was Annie Mae Hollis, a black woman who took care of the children when Miss Lillian was on nursing assignments. Annie Mae was the salt of the earth, good to the point of hurting, as even-tempered and uncomplaining a person as ever lived. She could not have loved the children more if they had been her own; and she would do anything and everything they asked of her. Her caring also extended to other members of the family. When Tom Gordy returned after the war, sick and emaciated, Annie Mae took it upon herself to look after him. "Tom loved it," Miss Lillian laughs fondly. "He went out of his way to be pampered. He would go walking off from the house, out to the very end of that field where all the pecan trees are. Then he would sit down and call out for Annie Mae to bring him something."

All of these people—members of an extended family—contributed toward the shaping of the Carter children. But the one strongest influence had to be Mr. Earl. Through his industry, enterprise, and hard work, he set an example for them. He also set an example through his involvement in civic and community affairs, taking on the task of local rural electrification in the thirties, serving on the county board of education and in the Georgia legislature. He also molded their habits in overtly insisting on good behavior and good moral conduct, and punishing them when they did not meet the high standards he set.

Earl Carter was adamant about lying. Whatever else he forgave—and he did forgive as well as punish—he would not tolerate a lie. The reason for this has never been suggested by anyone, but it may well go back to his father's tragic death. In that dispute over the desk, there had been accusations of lying.

"I know there's been a lot of talk about Jimmy not telling a lie," Miss Lillian offers seriously. "But there was one thing his father just could not stand, and that was a lie. When the children were older, Earl never whipped them for mischief, but he still whipped them if they told a lie. One time, he told Billy not to eat some pears which were green. When Earl caught him with a pear, Billy threw it away. Earl asked, 'Billy, were you eating a pear?' And Billy answered, 'No, Daddy.' Earl gave him a whipping for telling a lie. Earl couldn't stand a liar; to my knowledge, he never lied to me. And neither has Jimmy."

Miss Lillian's face can't stay serious for too long, however. Breaking into a broad grin, she adds, "I had a lady interviewing me, and she was from France, and she was being very difficult. She asked, 'Do you mean Jimmy *never* told a lie?' I answered, 'I imagine he told white lies.' She didn't understand what I meant and I explained, 'A white lie is like I told you this morning when I said you looked beautiful.'"

Miss Lillian laughs at herself—something she does regularly. She is never intentionally unkind, but sometimes she just can't ignore the truth, and she's the kind that says what's going on in her mind. She is an extraordinary woman, and she has reared an extraordinary brood of children, one of whom happens to be president of the United States.

But to Miss Lillian, Jimmy is no more special than her other children. In a way she's right; but, when she says, "Jimmy was a very *or*dinary child; he showed *no* potential," with that merry little twinkle in her eye, you recall how Jimmy described his childhood as one of poverty. And then you realize it's all relative; it all depends upon the viewpoint. To Miss Lillian, Jimmy is ordinary, just as she is ordinary.

Jimmy Carter's boyhood was not really that of a Mark Twain hero. Jimmy posed for this photograph as part of a class assignment for Miss Julia Coleman. Each of the students had to be photographed as a character in literature. Jimmy was Huck Finn. (Neyland, courtesy of the Carter family)

Jimmy and Rosalynn:

The Early Years

For a great many Americans, during much of the twentieth century, home was the place they left in order to make something of themselves. The pattern of homesteading new territory was over for young people. The new frontier had moved to the colleges and universities, where a man or woman could get the knowledge and the education to rise to the top in business, industry, and science.

Jimmy Carter was only one of the countless young people who left the farms of America in the thirties and forties and turned in a completely different direction from the paths their families had traveled for generations.

Jimmy Carter wanted an appointment to Annapolis—that was his dream—but he needed more education before he could enter the Naval Academy. The Sumter County schools' curriculum was limited and Jimmy spent a year at Georgia South-

western and another year at Georgia Tech before he was fully prepared.

Annapolis was Jimmy's goal from the day he began school. That single-mindedness of purpose is an important key to his character. It is probably what made him so much more serious than most of his friends and fellow students. And that seriousness in turn prompted his father to nickname him "Hotshot," which was quickly shortened to "Hot." Jimmy was obviously capable of great effort and concentration, and never lost sight of his purpose, despite the natural inclination toward fun and mischief that he exhibited as a youngster.

Jimmy showed an interest in girls and dating at an early age—thirteen, according to his mother's recollection. (He borrowed his father's pickup to go on his first date.) But somehow he managed not to get serious about any particular girl until he had his goal—Annapolis—firmly within his grasp.

Jimmy was able to commute to Georgia Southwestern while studying there, since

Rosalynn Smith in her high school formal gown with a bouquet of three dozen red roses.
(Neyland, courtesy of the Smith family)

Jimmy Carter at nineteen, when he was a student at Georgia Tech. The taxing science courses there prompted Jimmy to study harder than he had ever done before. It was, he recalled later, a much more difficult year than any of his years at Annapolis. (Neyland, courtesy of the Carter family)

the school is in Americus, only ten miles from Plains. But the year he went to Georgia Tech, Jimmy moved away from home. It was not a very big move, and at the time, it seemed only temporary, but Jimmy would not be returning to Plains, except as a visitor, for the next eleven years.

While Jimmy was at Georgia Tech, he and his family remained in touch through frequent letters. Gloria was always the best correspondent, even if she was still just a youngster. Addressing him as "Hot," she signed her letters as either Gloria or Gogo. Jimmy apparently endured some teasing from his classmates about a secret sweetheart, because, as soon as he arrived at Annapolis, he wrote to Gloria with a request: "Dear Gloria, Please do not call me

'Hot,' and please do not write to me on lined notebook paper with pencil." The family laughs about that letter now, but at the time, Jimmy must have felt deeply about the matter. He was virtually incarcerated in an all-male school, where girls were a principal subject of conversation. Getting to be known around the campus as "Hot" would have been far more embarrassing than confessing to "lusting in one's heart."

During the first years at Annapolis, Jimmy channeled all his energy into school and his studies. He knew that he was not only getting a "free" education, but also building the foundations for a job and a career. The fact that it was wartime only reinforced the importance of what he was being taught: the knowledge he was gaining might one day mean the difference between life and death.

But when Jimmy decided he was ready to think about girls again, he acted—and acted decisively. No one knows exactly when or how Jimmy Carter first met

Plains High School was built in the 1920s, but the trees around the school were planted gradually over the years—a new one each time a future student was born in the town. (Neyland, courtesy of the Carter family)

Jimmy Carter's high school graduating class. Jimmy is crouching at the right. Jimmy never became too serious about any of the girls in high school, but the closest to being a "steady" was Teenie Ratliff, the girl seated on the ground closest to Jimmy in the picture. She later married Lonnie Taylor, the boy directly behind her. (Neyland, courtesy of the Carter family)

Jimmy Carter, home on a brief visit from Georgia Tech, took his brother Billy for a boat ride. Despite the wide differences in their ages and personalities, there is great affection between the brothers. Today, when asked if he objects to some of Billy's statements to the press, Jimmy has answered, "Nothing Billy would ever say could hurt me." Billy, when asked a similar question, answered, "I don't tell him how to run the country, and he doesn't tell me how to run the peanut business." (Neyland, courtesy of the Carter family)

Rosalynn Smith. In a town the size of Plains everybody automatically knows everybody else and Jimmy must have glimpsed Rosalynn numerous times without really noticing her.

It was in the summer of 1945 that Rosalynn first attracted Jimmy's attention. She was about to turn eighteen, and he was back in Plains for summer vacation before his last year at Annapolis. As he describes the event, he was "cruising around in a rumble-seated Ford with a friend," late one summer afternoon. ("Cruising" was just about the only activity there was for young people in the small town.) The two boys were on Church Street, which is also Highway 27. As they passed the Plains Methodist Church, near Grandmother Nina's house, they noticed two girls. One of the girls was Jimmy's sister Ruth, so they stopped to talk.

The other was a quiet, shy girl with a warm, dimpled smile and intelligent deep green eyes. Jimmy knew Rosalynn Smith had been a friend of Ruth's for years; and she lived just across town at the point where the road to Dawson and the road to Smithville meet. Maybe it was because she was a friend of his kid sister and three years younger than he was, but he had never really noticed her before. Now on the point of entering Georgia Southwestern to study interior decorating, Rosalynn struck him as a beautiful young woman. He asked her to go to the movies with him that evening.

James Earl Carter, Jr.

PLAINS, GEORGIA

During plebe year Jimmy spent a large part of his time learning songs for the first classmen, but the only time he raised his voice after that was to shout, "Brace up!" or "Square that cap!" Studies never bothered Jimmy. In fact, the only times he opened his books were when his classmates desired help on problems. This lack of study did not, however, prevent him from standing in the upper part of his class. Jimmy's many friends will remember him for his cheerful disposition and his ability to see the humorous side of any situation.

Jimmy no longer recalls whether the movie was any good. He does remember that when he got home from the movies, his mother asked what he thought of Rosalynn, and he answered immediately. "She's the girl I want to marry."

Making that decision was easy; getting Rosalynn to agree was more difficult. In December, when he came home for the Christmas holidays, he proposed. But Rosalynn said, "No." After all, she was just beginning college, and he would be graduating from the Naval Academy in a

Jimmy Carter as a plebe at Annapolis (Courtesy of the Annapolis Yearbook)

Midshipman James Earl Carter, Jr. in 1946, about the time Jimmy "met" Rosalynn. According to Miss Allie, Rosallynn's mother, her first impression was that Jimmy's uniform and his perfect white teeth made him irresistible. (Neyland, courtesy of the Carter family)

The Plains Methodist Church, where Jimmy asked Rosalynn for their first date and where Jimmy and Rosalynn were eventually married, almost a year later. Although Rosalynn changed from the Methodist to the Baptist faith, she and Jimmy occasionally still attend services at the Methodist Church in Plains. (Neyland)

Jimmy and Rosalynn, after their wedding, prepare to leave Plains. For all Jimmy's concern with punctuality, he and Rosalynn were both late for the wedding ceremony. To his dismay, when they arrived at the churchyard, the organist was already halfway through the wedding march. They had to wait for the organist to finish and start through a second time. (Neyland, courtesy of the Carter family)

always disarming. American novels and plays are filled with efforts to understand or explain the phenomenon of the Southern woman. But, whether it is Scarlett O'Hara or Melanie Wilkes, Regina Giddens or Blanche Dubois, they always seem to be portrayed as either predatory or insipidly stupid. Actually the true Southern woman is neither.

Two seemingly contradictory qualities —strength and gentleness—were essentials for the Southern frontierswoman. Strength was essential because frontier life was hard, and women had to be equal partners with their men in working the farm and plantation. Gentleness was important because the woman also had to guide the children's growth, as well as to provide a quiet haven in the home. These qualities are no longer so necessary in a modern urbanized society, but the times

Jimmy with his sister Ruth at his graduation from Annapolis. (Neyland, courtesy of the Carter family)

few months. But Jimmy was not to be put off easily. In the spring, when Rosalynn went north to Annapolis for a weekend, he asked again. This time, she said "yes," and they were married in a simple ceremony on July 7, 1946, at the Plains Methodist Church.

Today, the bond between Jimmy and Rosalynn is as strong as human love can be. After more than thirty years of marriage, the looks they exchange when they're out of the public eye remind one of a young couple still on their honeymoon.

Miss Allie, Rosalynn's mother, insists that Rosalynn was an ordinary girl, with an ordinary childhood. And, on first glance, that's what she appears to be—pretty, but ordinary. This is undoubtedly the result of her quiet, unassuming manner. It is when she speaks, however, that the *extraordinary* Rosalynn appears.

The Southern woman of intelligence is

On Graduation Day at Annapolis, Jimmy is flanked by Rosalynn (left) and Miss Lillian (right), the two most important women in his life. (Neyland, courtesy of the Carter family)

have changed more rapidly than the culture or the people.

Rosalynn Smith grew up in a manner only slightly different from the manner in which her mother and her grandmother were reared. Perhaps the only significant difference was that Rosalynn grew up in the town of Plains and Miss Allie grew up on the Murray farm a few miles outside of town.

In some ways Rosalynn's forebears, the Smiths and the Murrays, were very different from the Carters and the Gordys, but their general history and migration were much the same. The Smiths were from Marion County, Georgia, and had been there for some time. The Murrays, Miss Allie's family, had been on the same land in Sumter County for five generations. The Carters now own that land as a part of their farm; their children will be the sixth generation.

The first of Rosalynn's family to settle that land outside Plains was Druary Murray, born in North Carolina in 1787, and he arrived there as soon as the territory was opened up. The Murray home and the Murray cemetery are still there, nestled on either side of a quiet red dirt road. The house is a bit run down now and definitely

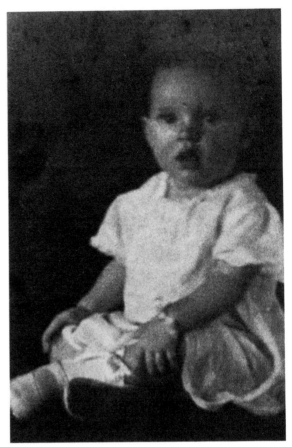

Miss Allie holding the infant Rosalynn. "An ordinary child," Miss Allie recalls. (Neyland, courtesy of the Smith family)

Rosalynn as a baby—a plump, unsmiling, serious little girl. (Neyland, courtesy of the Smith family)

needs painting, but it is clearly a comfortable home, unpretentious but functional.

Miss Allie was the only child of John William Murray, known as "Captain Murray," and Rosa Nettie Wise Murray. They were Methodists, which in the South is not much different from being Baptists, though each group likes to think of itself as just a little better than the other.

Miss Allie is not the sort of person to describe her childhood as lonely. She is not the sort who would ever feel sorry for herself. But one suspects she must have found it just a bit lonesome growing up in such quiet surroundings, as an only child. And that early isolation must account, in part, for her shyness.

Perhaps "shyness" is the wrong word, because it implies an awkwardness, and

there is nothing awkward or ill at ease about Miss Allie. Possibly "reserved" is the more appropriate word. Miss Allie *is* reserved, though she is also gracious. A "lady" is what most of the people in Plains call her. "Now *that*," they say, "is a lady. A genuine lady."

Meeting a "lady" in this day and age can be disconcerting, and it takes some getting used to. For one thing, you have to listen very carefully, because she speaks softly and slowly. And for another, you have to look at her when she is speaking or you're liable to miss something in her eyes or in her smile. You might also miss the fact that a "lady" can have strength, because she doesn't talk about it. But the strength is there. It shows up when she needs it.

Wilburn Edgar Smith, Rosalynn's father,

was a handsome and intelligent man. But he was a garage mechanic, a "grease monkey" as they call them in the South, and he worked hard to make a living for his family. Even before Mr. Edgar died, Miss Allie occasionally did sewing to help with finances. After he died in 1940, Miss Allie promptly went out to work to support the four children. Mr. Edgar had put aside some money to pay for the children's college education, but Miss Allie refused to touch that. Her first job was in a grocery store; she also continued to take in sewing from time to time. Later she got a job in the post office, where she worked until she reached retirement age. It was a heavy burden to carry, working full time, and trying to serve as both mother and father to a

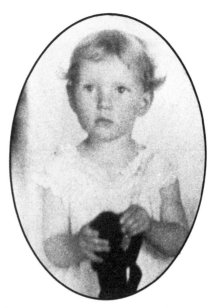

Rosalynn at about age five with a favorite stuffed animal—still unsmiling and serious, with inquisitive, intelligent eyes. (Neyland, courtesy of the Smith family)

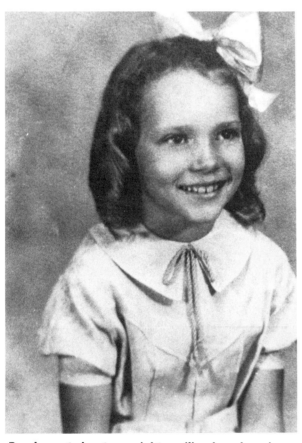

Rosalynn at about age eight, smiling her charming smile at last. Miss Allie recalls that others always marveled that Rosalynn could end up the day as neat and clean as she had begun it, her clothes unwrinkled and unsoiled. (Neyland, courtesy of the Smith family)

brood of young children. But that was what she had to do, and she did it without complaining. When Miss Allie's mother died, she had to assume the added responsibility of caring for her father, already something of an invalid at seventy-four, but destined to survive for another twenty-one years.

As the oldest of the Smith children, Rosalynn was forced to take on some of the responsibility of looking after her brothers, Jerry and Murray, and her sister, Alethea. So the necessity for strength, hard work, and seriousness fell early on Rosalynn. While there was not much time for parties, she still had a great many friends; she went to the movies, and she enjoyed dancing, either to phonograph records at home or at school functions. She was, as her mother describes her, an ordinary girl.

After the simple wedding ceremony at the Plains Methodist Church, Rosalynn set off with her husband for the naval base at Norfolk, Virginia, where Jimmy was assigned to duty. The life she entered was quite different from the life of Plains, but the resources of her upbringing came into their own. In the seven years of Jimmy's

Rosalynn's great-great-grandfather, Druary Murray, built this log cabin in 1863 for Rosalynn's great-grandfather, John William Fulwood Murray, as a wedding present. It continued to stand until recent years on the family land five miles south of Plains. (Neyland, courtesy of Mrs. Beth Walters)

The Murray home today, minus a part of its original porch. (Neyland)

Rosalynn's father's parents, Wilburn Juriston Smith and Sarah Eleanor Bell Smith. (Neyland, courtesy of the Smith family)

Members of the Murray family gathered for a family reunion. (Neyland, courtesy of Mrs. Beth Walters)

Rosalynn's grandfather, John William Murray, as a young man. Though never in the military, he was known as "Captain." Jimmy and Rosalynn named their first son Jack for him. (Neyland, courtesy of the Smith family)

Rosalynn's father, Wilburn Edgar Smith. A handsome, sensitive, intelligent man, he worked hard in the hope that his children would have the education and opportunities that he had missed. When he died at forty-four, he left money that he insisted be used to send his children to college. All four fulfilled his request. Right: Miss Allie in the 1920s, a very ladylike flapper. (Neyland, courtesy of the Smith family)

The Murray homestead remains much as it was fifty years ago when Miss Allie lived there. The road, still unpaved, separates the house from the outbuildings and the family cemetery. (Neyland)

Miss Allie as a child, her shyness appearing more as coquettishness. The neatness and the prettiness that would later show up in Rosalynn are already apparent in her mother. (Neyland, courtesy of the Smith family)

naval career, he and Rosalynn lived in many different places, among people whose backgrounds were very different from theirs. There were many adjustments to be made, but as they moved from place to place, they began to see similarities in people as well as differences. Whether it was Virginia or Connecticut, Hawaii or California, people were basically the same. Only some of the customs were different.

There were times when Jimmy and Rosalynn saw little of each other. In fact, during the first two years of his service, while Jimmy was assigned to the U.S.S. *Wyoming* and the U.S.S. *Mississippi*, he was able to spend only four to six days of every month with Rosalynn—only two out of every three weekends. The rest of the time he was at sea.

The major adjustment was not Jimmy's, but Rosalynn's. During the years at Annapolis, Jimmy had gone on summer training cruises; he knew what to expect. But Rosalynn had to spend her time alone in the apartment in Norfolk, and she had to manage on Jimmy's limited pay. After the rent was paid, Rosalynn had $71 a month left over for everything else.

But to Jimmy, every experience was a challenge, and after a while Rosalynn began to see it that way too. While Jimmy was at sea, experimenting with new radar and equipment, and training enlisted men, Rosalynn was learning to manage money. And, after the first year of marriage, she was meeting the challenge of parenthood—alone, much of the time. Four days before their first wedding anniversary, Jimmy and Rosalynn became the parents of a baby boy—John William Carter, named for Rosalynn's grandfather. The new parents called him Jack.

With the end of his two-year duty, Jimmy reached the decisive moment when he had to choose a direction for his naval career. He chose submarine duty, and, as in all his previous decisions, Jimmy chose well. He looked upon this new area of service as a challenge, and it so happened the challenge helped him move rapidly to success.

He and Rosalynn and Jack moved to New London, Connecticut, for his six months at the officers' training school there. When the training was concluded in December, 1948, the family went home to Plains before shipping out to Hawaii. Jimmy went on ahead aboard his first submarine, the U.S.S. *Pomfret;* Rosalynn followed with Jack. It was on that first trip across the Pacific that Jimmy almost lost his life: the sub was surfaced, and Jimmy was on deck when a giant wave struck the ship and he was washed thirty feet aft. Had the ship been at a slightly different angle, Jimmy would have been lost at sea.

In Hawaii, on April 12, 1950, a second son was born to the Carters, James Earl Carter III. The new baby was called "a chip off the old block" by the hospital nurses, thereby gaining the permanent nickname of Chip.

Soon after Chip was born, and after a brief stay in San Diego, Jimmy was ordered back to New London to work on the development of the U.S.S. *K–1,* a new type of submarine that used sonar detection. Because of his work on this small sub, Jimmy was then qualified to command submarines. As it turned out, he did not remain in the Navy long enough to get one assigned to him.

After four years of marriage and four years of naval life, things were really beginning to look good for the Jimmy Carters and their two children. Jimmy seemed to excel at whatever he undertook, and they had no doubt that he could go all the way to the top. Rosalynn had learned how to manage money; she had found friends among the other Navy wives; and she was enjoying the challenge of raising her young children. It was during this period in Connecticut that their third son, Donnel Jeffrey Carter (called Jeff) was born on August 18, 1952.

Jimmy applied for assignment to the nuclear submarine development program and was accepted. But he had first to con-

Rosalynn's sister, Lillian Alethea Smith, as a young woman. The Smiths and Carters were already close. Alethea was named for Miss Lillian and for her mother. Alethea is married to Lee Wall and lives in Ellenwood, Georgia. (Neyland, courtesy of the Smith family)

front a question that was to be one of the most important of his life. To be accepted into the nuclear submarine program, Jimmy had to pass an interview with Captain Hyman Rickover, the man who would be his immediate superior. Jimmy tried to impress the captain with his knowledge of a wide range of subjects—current events, music, literature, and electronics, amongst others. But with each turn, Rickover made him feel he knew less and less. Finally, the applicant was asked about his standing at the Naval Academy.

Proud of his high standing, Jimmy answered, "Sir, I stood fifty-ninth in a class of eight hundred and twenty."

"Did you do your best?" Rickover asked.

Jimmy started to answer "yes," but changed his mind. "No, sir," he responded suddenly.

"Why not?" Rickover wanted to know.

It was a question Jimmy could not answer. He passed the interview, apparently answering Rickover's questions better than he thought, but that last question: Why not the best? struck a sensitive nerve. It continued to bother him. From the time he had earned his nickname of "Hotshot," Jimmy had prided himself on working hard and excelling at whatever he did. He had thought of excelling in terms of competition with others; but he had never thought of competing with himself—doing the very best that *he* could do. From that day forward, his standard for judging himself changed. He never again measured his own achievements against those of others; he judged himself only by his own incredibly high standards.

Jimmy admired Rickover, perhaps looked up to him the way he had once looked up to Uncle Tom Gordy. The captain, who eventually became an admiral, had stamina, determination, and perseverance. He was tough and hard-working. These were qualities Jimmy Carter also had in some degree, but he wanted to develop them even further.

He threw himself into his work on the nuclear submarine; he was teaching, demonstrating, experimenting, and researching during the day. At night he was taking courses in nuclear physics. He often said jokingly that his great ambition in the Navy was to be Chief of Naval Operations. For him, at one time, that was the best. But soon he would have to step back and judge himself in another light: Chief of Naval Operations might be the best among his peers, but was it the best that *he* could do? He was meeting great challenges in the nuclear submarine program, but was he truly meeting the standards he set himself?

That question would not arise until 1953. After more than six years of marriage, Jimmy and Rosalynn had adjusted happily to their nomadic life. It was a life filled with challenges for both of them. Like most people who leave the farms and small towns of America to do new and exciting things, they must occasionally have looked back nostalgically at the tranquil, settled, easygoing life they had left. But never would they have considered going back to that life—not for a minute.

On a trip back to Plains, Jimmy pauses for a picture with family and friends. Front row, left to right: Ruth, Gloria, Billy, Nina Pratt with her daughter, Ruth Carter (Hugh's wife) with Hugh, Jr. Second row, left to right: Don Carter, Jimmy, and Willard Slappey. (Neyland, courtesy of the Carter family)

You Must Go Home Again

In any Southern community, there are likely to be many people with the same last name. In Plains, there are several Mr. Carters, and several Mrs. Carters. Calling a man or a woman by his or her given name is not just a sign of familiarity; it also makes it easier to differentiate one person from the other. The practice does not imply any lack of respect; on the contrary, it provides for a variation that signifies the highest regard. Traditionally, a man who had earned great respect in the community would have "Mister" added to his first name, and a woman held in high regard would be called "Miss," whether she was married or not.

Mr. Earl and Miss Lillian were highly respected persons in Sumter County. They were persons of authority, and they were also, in a way, parental figures to more than just those in their immediate family. They were people to whom anyone in the community could come if he or she were in trouble or in need of help. It didn't matter what the problems were—finances, serious illness, legal questions, marital disputes—either or both of the Carters, Mr. Earl or Miss Lillian, would be able to assist those in need. Time and again they showed that they were people who cared about other people.

Mr. Earl had built up a large and successful peanut farm from only a few hundred acres, letting out some of his land to sharecroppers and hiring farmworkers to assist him in the planting and harvesting of the rest. Because a farmer's success depended upon the ability to sell quickly and easily, Mr. Earl saw the need for a peanut warehouse in Plains, and he established one there, buying and selling his neighbors' produce as well as his own.

Farming involves much more than simply having something in the ground; it also involves the ability of the farmer to get it out of the ground and to market. The farmer's health, his family problems, and his financial status can often interfere with that. In this way, Mr. Earl's position was a paternalistic one and his responsibility toward the other farmers extended far beyond the buying and selling of peanuts.

Mr. Earl worked on the farm and in the warehouse from sunrise to sunset, and often spent his evenings involved in community responsibilities—with the school board or representing Sumter County in the Georgia legislature. Miss Lillian worked hard too. She nursed the sick, looked after the home, and cooked the meals. "One thing Earl always insisted on," she remembers, "was having a hot meal every night. And he always had to have his hoecake of cornbread. Some nights we'd have steak, some we'd have pork, but we'd always have that cornbread."

By 1949, the Carters had moved out of the house at Archery, and into an attractive red brick home in Plains. Jimmy and Gloria had grown up and left the fold. Ruth was just about grown, and she would soon be leaving home as well. The neat, modern, compact house in town was much more practical for Mr. Earl, Miss Lillian, and Billy. And it may have been that Mr. Earl knew he wouldn't be around much longer. He had cancer of the pancreas.

At the end of 1952, when Jimmy learned that his father was dying of cancer, he requested and received an extended leave to go home to Plains to be with his parents. His position was a complex one, and he had difficult questions to face. It was easy enough to get leave and to travel to Plains for a short stay, but he was not quite prepared for the implications of his father's death and his own return home.

Mr. Earl's death was a difficult and a painful one, but Jimmy sat with his father, and shared the pain and agony. He was the oldest son; there had always been a certain responsibility in that. But, until now, his principal responsibility had been to himself, and to his wife and children. Since his graduation from high school, he had lived his own life independently, away from Plains and his parents. The possibility of returning to that society had never occurred to him. But the time spent at his father's deathbed became a time of contemplation.

Jimmy loved and respected his father. Mr. Earl was a good man, and his life had had meaning—tangible, visible meaning in its effect upon the lives of those around him. The values that Mr. Earl represented were strict and unwavering; they were conservative values, which did not allow for great social changes; and consequently

Mr. Earl's grave, a simple headstone. (Neyland)

The headstone of the Carter plot at the Plains cemetery, where Mr. Earl was buried in 1953. (Neyland)

he and Jimmy had some minor political differences. But Mr. Earl was also a loving and caring man, and Jimmy knew that he and Billy and Gloria and Ruth had often turned to him with their troubles or concerns—just as the neighbors, both black and white, had done. And Mr. Earl had always been there when he was needed.

The Carter family in one of its rare moments together after the death of Mr. Earl. (Neyland, courtesy of the Carter family)

This was a strong contrast to Jimmy's own life. Compared with his father's life, Jimmy's was a selfish one. There was challenge and there was excitement in the Navy, and there was a chance for prestige and importance. But whatever good he was doing was an abstract good. And, as far as affecting the lives of those closest to him, Jimmy knew that he was little more than a part-time husband and father.

When Mr. Earl died, the neighbors— black and white—came to pay their respects. There is nothing like a funeral to make a man weigh himself and judge the relative merits of his own life.

The decision to return to Plains was Jimmy's, and Jimmy's alone. Rosalynn did not want him to give up his naval career; she did not want to go home—that is, not to stay. After their education, their extensive travel, and the sophistication and challenge of their way of life, returning to the farm just didn't seem possible.

But there was the problem of the family business. Billy wasn't yet old enough to take over. Miss Lillian was a strong and talented woman, but she was not a businesswoman. And Jimmy's sisters had their own concerns. Unless Jimmy returned to manage the business, there were only two alternatives: either hire someone to run it, or sell it. Either of those alternatives would mean forsaking his family and the other farmers of Sumter County.

For some reason, a great many people assume that Miss Lillian demanded that Jimmy return home to take over the business. It did not happen that way. The deciding factor was Jimmy's realization that he had to make his life amount to something in human terms.

Jimmy and Rosalynn also felt the responsibility of caring for their widowed mothers, but that was not a deciding fac-

tor. As it turned out, neither mother became a burden. Miss Allie continued to work and support herself as she always had. And anyone who thinks Miss Lillian is a domineering mother is quite wrong. There is a great difference between a strong mother and a domineering one. A domineering mother is possessive and generally feigns weakness and frailty to get her way. A strong mother is an independent woman who leads her own life and lets her children lead theirs. Miss Lillian is the strong, independent type. Soon after Jimmy and Rosalynn returned to Plains, Miss Lillian left to find a new life for herself, taking a job as housemother to the Kappa Alpha fraternity at Auburn University.

"It wasn't that I needed the money," Miss Lillian explains. "It was because I couldn't allow myself to sit at home and grieve over Earl's death. If I had, I would have just given up living completely. When I took the job, my children were very concerned about me. They didn't want it to appear that I took the job because I *needed* it—they bought me a brand-new car so I could arrive at the KA house in style."

The Carters were by no means poor, but there was not a superabundance of money in the Carter company when Jimmy and Rosalynn returned to take over. There are good and bad years in the peanut business, and 1954 was one of the worst. Because of the drought that year, they ended up with a profit of $187. Jimmy ran the company, making the decisions and supplying all the brawn as well, spending much of his time loading trucks. Rosalynn served as the accountant, keeping the books. Miss Lillian was a silent partner and investor. But, with so small a profit in 1954, there was nowhere to go but up. And Jimmy soon had the business growing and expanding.

When Jimmy and Rosalynn and their three sons moved back to Plains, they had to take an apartment in the public housing

Miss Lillian's home in Plains today. It is an unpretentious house of contemporary design. Miss Lillian lives there alone with her dog, Periwinkle, a beautiful brown standard poodle allowed to run free about Plains until someone took his collar as a souvenir. (Neyland)

Miss Allie and Miss Lillian, two beautiful and admirable ladies, but with two extremely different personalities, each independent and strong in her own way. (Neyland)

development, until they could afford to rent a house or to buy one. The public housing in Plains consists of a series of small, red-brick duplexes, covering approximately half a block. They are not unattractive buildings, and as public housing goes, they have been well kept up and maintained; but they are not particularly comfortable or spacious for a family of five. As soon as Jimmy and Rosalynn were able, they took a house outside town on the Archery road. It is a comfortable, old-fashioned house that some in Plains claim to be haunted, though none of the Carters

ever noticed anything unusual about the place.

The first years that Jimmy and Rosalynn spent back in Plains were years of adjustment, and (that favorite Carter phrase) years of challenge. Because methods of farming had changed since he had left the farm, Jimmy found it necessary to take courses at the Agricultural Experiment Station in Tifton. And Rosalynn took courses in accounting in order to learn to keep her four separate sets of accounts for the business.

There was also a challenge in adapting

The Carters' first home upon their return to Plains was a little cramped for a family of five—Apartment 9A in the public housing project. On their way home, the Carters stopped off in Washington to see their congressman, who began complaining about "the terrible people who live in public housing," not knowing where the Carters intended to live. (Neyland

The house on the Archery road where Jimmy and Rosalynn lived after they could afford to move from the public housing. Today, some in Plains claim that this house is haunted, but none of the Carters ever saw evidence of spirits there. (Neyland)

themselves to the small-town social life. But they made friends easily, and there were a number of people in their age group with a degree of education and sophistication, so that adjustment was made more easily than they had expected. People entertained in their homes, and there was a place in Albany, not too far away, where they and their friends could go dancing. Rosalynn still enjoyed dancing just as much as she had as a teenager.

Jimmy joined the local Lions Club and found a place for himself on the school board. Since one of the reasons for his decision to return to Plains was his desire to live in a community in which he could accomplish tangible benefits, he began to look about him to see what the community needed. Summers can grow very hot in Plains, Georgia, and it occurred to him that the young people could certainly use a place to go swimming. So Jimmy stirred up the energies of the Lions Club, and they raised the funds to build a pool.

Assuming leadership in a Southern community in the late fifties could also have its problems—particularly if the leader had a conscience and a belief in equality. This was the time of the Supreme Court decision on the integration of the public schools, and the time of Southern whites' backlash against any kind of change in "their" society.

During the late fifties and early sixties, because of the manner in which television and newspaper reports highlighted the news, it may have appeared that there were only two kinds of people in the South: the militant revolutionaries and the staunch white supremacists. But that was not the case; there were as many different kinds of people in the South as there are anywhere else in the country. And the South would not have survived that period if it had not been for people like Jimmy Carter. He existed within the established framework, within "the system," and yet he believed the changes were right and just. He did not speak out loudly and stridently or march with a picket sign, but his actions spoke to his neighbors as effectively as any speech.

When a White Citizens Council formed in Plains, Jimmy refused to join. When it was pointed out to him that every other white business leader had joined, he still refused. He continued to refuse even after a boycott was organized against his business. At the time, Jimmy was apprehensive but he knew he was taking the right course and he refused to be influenced by fear. It may have been that he also knew that most of his neighbors were basically good people who would soon realize that the objectives of the Citizens Council were wrong. Whether Jimmy foresaw it or not, the boycott of his business didn't hold. Most of his neighbors soon realized that they had behaved irrationally, through fear and insecurity.

As Jimmy's mother had always been an example to her children, conveying a belief in right and wrong through her actions more than her words, Jimmy now conveyed simple justice and truth to his neighbors through his example. He was one of many people in business and civic organizations throughout the South who made peaceful changes possible.

Even if there had been nothing else to justify Jimmy's decision to return to Plains, this one experience was some kind of confirmation. Jimmy belonged in Plains because he had grown up there and knew and loved his neighbors. Yet he had had education and experiences that went far beyond those of the average farmer. A man who left home had to change; but home could also change. And, if a man truly loved his home—his family and his friends and neighbors—he had to ignore Thomas Wolfe's advice. He *had* to go home again. A man must put back into his society as

On her return to Plains, Rosalynn became accustomed to busy working days, whether keeping books for the Carter Warehouse or looking after her home and family. Here, she rakes leaves in front of the elegant Carter home on Woodland Drive. *(Atlanta Journal-Constitution)*

The entrance to the Carter Warehouse itself—down a back alley behind the telephone company. (Neyland)

Jimmy Carter unloading peanuts at the Carter Warehouse. Although this is a recent photograph, it demonstrates the kind of work he did after he left the Navy to return to Plains. (Wide World)

Jimmy explains to reporters the different parts of the peanut plant. Until Jimmy became a presidential candidate, most Americans thought the nut grew above ground. (UPI)

The offices of the Carter Warehouse today. The offices are now run by Billy and Sybil Carter. Most people agree that the phenomenal success of the Carter Warehouse has been due to the "good ol' boy," who hides an excellent business mind behind his beer-drinking exterior. (Neyland)

Billy and Jimmy. Shortly after Jimmy and Rosalynn returned to Plains, Billy left to go to college and into the Marine Corps. However, when Jimmy went into politics, Billy returned to take over the family business. (Neyland, courtesy of the Carter family)

Gloria Carter, after a brief time away from Plains, returned and married a farmer, Walter Spann. Despite her claim of being a simple farmer's wife, Gloria is an intelligent, sophisticated woman. For many years a teacher of art, she has taken easily to writing—beginning with letters to her brother "Hot," going on to magazine articles, and to a sensitive book about her mother's years in India. Here Gloria rides a tractor but the public is more accustomed to seeing her on her motorcycle. (Wide World)

much as he has taken out—and more. He has to grow with his home and permit it to grow with him.

The next stage in the growth of Jimmy Carter was his participation in local politics, following the pattern of his father and his grandfather Gordy who had been similarly involved out of an attitude of service to their community. For Jimmy, the decision was an important one, because he would have to give up his responsibilities in the family business, and turn the company over to brother Billy, who had now finished his education and was out of the Marine Corps.

Jimmy felt he could be of benefit to his community and to his state, but he decided to discuss the matter with a minister who was visiting in Plains. The clergyman was opposed to the idea. Politics was a dirty business, he felt, and a good man could not stay in politics for long without being totally corrupted by it.

"If you want to be of service to other people," he suggested, "why don't you go into the ministry or some honorable social service work?" Jimmy's answer was, "How would you like to be the minister of a church with 80,000 members?"

Jimmy decided to run for the state legislature. His decision would prove to be a challenge, not only to him and Rosalynn, but to the whole family. It was 1962, and he entered the race for the Democratic nomination late, so he had to work harder than his opponents.

He set up a rigorous schedule of campaign appearances in all the towns and villages of the district. For speed and efficiency, he did a large part of his traveling by motorbike. His campaign style, set in this first race, was the same style that would eventually take him to the White House. His approach was to go directly to the people, to seek out the individual voters rather than to try to take over political machines.

Again, the greater challenge was for Rosalynn; she had to strive to overcome

Jimmy with his sister Ruth Carter Stapleton. When Jimmy and Rosalynn returned to Plains, Ruth had already left to live in North Carolina. (Wide World)

The Billy Carter home in Plains. When each of his children reaches fifteen, Billy gives that one a car. So far three have reached fifteen. With the birth of baby Earl (number six), the Carters have decided to build a much larger home. (Neyland)

her shyness; she did not campaign the way she would in later years, but she still had to speak in public and she had to entertain strangers in her home. She also had to take on some of the responsibilities of business and politics for which Jimmy didn't have time.

Both met the challenges well.

Jimmy met the problem of political corruption head-on. His opponent was the candidate of the local party machine. On election day, Jimmy visited the polls. In one county, the county political boss was standing at the polls actually forcing the voters to vote for his candidate. When Jimmy witnessed the man actually changing a woman's vote himself, Jimmy protested. But his protests were ignored. Jimmy wanted to visit the polls in other

Left: **Friends of the Carters, Ralph and Dollie Cornwell. After Jimmy returned home, he and Ralph often went hunting together.**
Center: **Maxine Reese has long been a friend of the Carters in Plains. Formerly a schoolteacher, she now manages the tourism to Plains and any request to see or speak to a member of the Carter family.**
Right: **Mattie Beth and William Spires in front of the Plains Pharmacy, where Mattie Beth works. William Spires is Billy Carter's father-in-law; he married Mattie Beth after Sybil's mother died. When Jimmy announced his candidacy for the presidency, William Spires was confronted with a problem: one of his best friends was George Wallace. However, Jimmy solved that dilemma by winning the primaries.** (Neyland)

counties, so he recruited his friend John Pope to look after the problem at the Quitman County polls.

When the election returns came in, Jimmy was defeated by the vote in Quitman County. But Jimmy and John Pope had proof that the ballot box there had been stuffed. By watching the polls, they knew that only about three hundred people had voted; but the ballot box contained four hundred and thirty-three ballots, many of them in the name of people who were dead, in prison, or now residing in some other county. Many of the ballots, when counted, proved not to have been folded up individually, but in groups of four, six, and eight; and an amazing number of people had voted in perfect alphabetical order.

By collecting affidavits from voters, Jimmy came up with an irrefutable court case. In court, the Quitman County vote was thrown out, and Jimmy was declared the winner of the Democratic nomination —almost.

There was a new state law that permitted appeal to the local Democratic Executive Committee, and of course that was dominated by the backers of Jimmy's opponent. Jimmy was again defeated, but he quickly appealed to the state party chairman; finally, Jimmy had won. But it was only the nomination; there was still the race against the Republican opponent. However, compared with what he had faced within his own party, that would be an easy victory.

That first experience in politics had a profound effect on Jimmy. Already concerned that certain groups of people could form and deprive others of their rights, he now saw very clearly and very personally the way these groups operated.

In his book, *Why Not the Best?*, he described what he had learned:

I began to realize how vulnerable our political system was to an accumulation of unchallenged power. Honest and courageous people could be quieted when they came to realize that outspoken opposition was fruitless. Those who were timid and insecure could be intimidated. The dishonest could band together to produce and divide the spoils, and they could easily elect officials who most often seemed respectable but who would cooperate in order to gain a title or office. Jury lists and voter lists could be controlled. Welfare recipients and other dependent people would be aided or deprived. Political favors could be delivered to high officials. And local news media sometimes looked the other way.

This realization has stayed with him, and in his career as an elected official, he has refused to tie himself too closely to special interest groups. To maintain his commitment to the people, he has refused even to define himself too strictly as either a liberal or a conservative. He remains a populist, with perhaps more liberal leanings than conservative ones. He has welcomed the support of groups, but has never committed himself to serving their interests.

During his two terms in the Georgia legislature, Jimmy worked tirelessly against any bill that would serve only special interests and for any that would be of benefit to the people. He does admit that the work proved to be more than he had expected; upon taking office, he had promised to read each and every bill that was brought forth for consideration, not realizing that there could be as many as 2,500 bills and resolutions in each forty-day session. But Jimmy was a man of his word; he took a speed-reading course and managed to live up to his promise.

Jimmy was not inclined toward self-praise. But he had managed to do an amazing thing: he had returned home to a small Georgia town, and he had managed to serve his community while preserving his own ideals and special insights. Now he saw that his community had expanded beyond the confines of Sumter County, but he still maintained that integrity.

His fellow legislators were people like those he had known for most of his life.

With few exceptions, most of them meant well; they were mostly good honest people trying to serve their constituencies. Yet many of them were often too short-sighted to see the full implications of some of the things they voted for and against. In many ways, the government of the state of Georgia had become like a blind man trying to analyze an elephant. The legislators considered every part of their work separately from every other part; the result was

Because of this photo, it has been supposed that Jimmy conducted his gubernatorial campaign on a motorbike. However, most of his traveling around the state was done by car. He managed to speak in every city, town, and village. (Courtesy of the Carter Campaign Headquarters)

waste, duplication, and inefficiency.

It seemed from the 1964 attempt to write a new state constitution, that some of the legislators did not even understand the very basics of the democratic form of government. The framers of that document could not even agree to approve the Bill of Rights of the U.S. Constitution, and they passed a requirement that every citizen *had* to worship God. By the time the document was finished, it was riddled with amendments designed to benefit various individuals and special interest groups.

Out of these astounding experiences, Jimmy Carter began to perceive the need for a strong and conscientious leader in his state government. The idea of a Jimmy Carter race for the governor's post began to take shape in his mind. With only two terms (four years) of experience in the legislature, Jimmy was relatively unknown in the state of Georgia. But he believed something had to be done, and he could see no one else to do it but him.

This decision was not reached so easily and so quickly as other decisions Jimmy had made. Trying to be practical, Jimmy thought it would be better to try for the U.S. Congress first, since he was not well known throughout Georgia. He declared himself a candidate for Congress in the spring of 1966; and he and Rosalynn and his sister Gloria began to write to people to ask about the issues that concerned them. But, during the campaign, friends and associates persuaded Jimmy to drop out of that race and enter the race for governor. With some reluctance and many doubts, Jimmy did.

This was the era of Lester Maddox and his ax-handle; it was the time of backlash in the state of Georgia. In the six-way race for the Democratic nomination, Jimmy was painted as the liberal and the heavy. The entire Carter family worked in Jimmy's campaign, and some of them had to endure considerable abuse. Rosalynn had overcome much of her shyness, but she was unable to harden herself against the unreasonable and venomous attacks. Miss Lillian was also a very visible target, who bore the brunt of the charges from outraged whites. In 1964, she had been in charge of Lyndon Johnson's campaign in Plains, and Johnson was being blamed for the race riots and rising welfare costs in the country. Miss Lillian had always been outspoken on equal rights, so she became a local focus of hatred.

"I didn't know that much about Lyndon

Number 1 Woodland Drive, the present home of Jimmy and Rosalynn Carter in Plains. The room visible on the left, among the trees, is Jimmy's study. (Neyland)

Jimmy in his study. (Wide World)

Johnson," she recalls now, "but when I began to get those ugly letters and phone calls, and when my car was smeared with soap, I fought for his election as hard as I could."

Another member of the family, Chip Carter, did not survive the Johnson campaign so staunchly. Only fourteen at the time, Chip had tried to wear his Lyndon Johnson button to school. After being beaten up and having his button torn off three times, Chip gave up and remained silent.

During the 1966 gubernatorial campaign, Jimmy was attacked for his belief in equal rights; and Lester Maddox was praised for carrying an ax-handle to beat up any blacks

who sought equality with whites. It was perhaps the most irrational election in Georgia since the end of Reconstruction.

Jimmy Carter received the most resounding defeat of his political career. His response was not bitterness, but it must have hurt. He had dedicated his life to helping the people, *all* of the people, and he had been rejected by them. For a short while, he considered giving up politics. But at that lowest point, when his courage and his faith in himself were almost gone, he experienced what has been called a "rebirth," and he returned to his commitment with twice the strength he had before. The next time he would not be defeated.

Born Again

There has been too much said and too little explained about Jimmy Carter's spiritual rebirth. The language of Southern Baptists is strangely like modern English, yet it is actually a foreign language to anyone not of the Baptist faith. It makes use of terms and phrases straight out of the King James Version of the Bible, and those terms and phrases have special, symbolic meanings only for someone who has sat through years of Sundays, listening to the dronings of Baptist preachers. It is a language that—for most of the American people—needs translation.

The Baptist faith has been much maligned. Oddly enough, the greatest failings of the faith are also its greatest virtues: a quality of simplicity, a stark and primitive distinction between good and evil, and a categorical listing of "Thou shalts" and "Thou shalt nots" that even the most lowly and uneducated can follow.

The Southern Baptist Convention is the second largest religious group in the United States, and it can probably be said that all of its members mean well, though not all are capable of practicing what they preach. By the sensitive and the intelligent, this is seen—perhaps justly—as hypocrisy; and the most sensitive and intelligent members of the Baptist church generally come to a moment of spiritual crisis. Many of them leave the church and become its harshest critics. A few have the strength and the courage to see that its failings are human, and choose to remain.

These few probably number in the thousands, but they are scattered among churches all over the country, and they are almost always in the minority in their congregations. They are probably among the finest practitioners of the Christian faith anywhere. They genuinely strive to be good and loving people. They are not always noticeable as Baptists, because they do not necessarily proselytize, but they put all of their energies into living according to the example of Christ.

Jimmy Carter is one of the best of Southern Baptists. His religion is a personal creed, not something to force on others. Whatever rigidity or judgment there may be, is applied only to himself. And when he judges someone else by his own standards, he usually admits later that it was a mistake, and that he did not live up to one part of his creed.

The story of Jimmy's spiritual rebirth has been told time and again, and it has done nothing but confuse most non-Baptists while sending Baptists into raptures of unwarranted hosannas.

For modern man, the verses of John 3:3–6 are almost incomprehensible. They state:

Jesus answered [Nicodemus] and said unto him, Verily, verily, I say unto thee, Except a man be born again, he cannot see the kingdom of God.

Nicodemus saith unto him, How can a man be born when he is old? can he enter the second time into his mother's womb, and be born?

Jesus answered, Verily, verily, I say unto thee, Except a man be born of water and of the Spirit, he cannot enter into the kingdom of God.

That which is born of the flesh is flesh; and that which is born of the Spirit is spirit.

For most born-again Baptists, the moment of rebirth comes after years of striving to live a good life, of trying to reconcile personal physical wants and needs with the spiritual requirements of their God. This rebirth can be of varying degrees of depth, depending upon the extremes of the physical and spiritual requirements, but it is always a profound experience. For that moment at least, the truth about their lives becomes clear.

However, it is not necessarily a mystical experience, nor as dramatic as Saul of Tar-

sus being struck off his horse by the blinding flash of light on the road to Damascus. Most often, it is a moment of quiet reflection, a moment not particularly memorable except for the self-realization.

Jimmy Carter does not remember his own spiritual rebirth, at least not in the wildly extravagant terms described by the press. He does recall, however, a moment of quiet reflection and spiritual regeneration.

Before his "rebirth," Jimmy Carter was already a "good" man. His greatest weaknesses were not terrible sins—they were ambition and a tendency toward pride. A minor personal crisis came when his ambition and pride received a severe blow, when he was defeated in his race for the governorship of Georgia. He had wanted desperately to win; outside his family, winning that election was probably the most important thing in the world to him.

Late in 1966, after his unsuccessful campaign, Jimmy's sister Ruth was visiting in Plains, and she and Jimmy went for a walk in the pinewoods outside town. They were talking about their thoughts, feelings, and experiences, the way all the members of the Carter family do among themselves.

For a long time Ruth had had problems, conflicts, and doubts in her life, but Jimmy could see that she had changed—that there were strength and peace in her now. At one time, Ruth had thought her problems were psychological, and she had sought resolution of them in group therapy. But, as it turned out, the problems were spiritual, and they were resolved through weekend retreats with a Christian fellowship group. In the peaceful, quiet surroundings, contemplating and sometimes sharing with the others questions she had about her life, she had found her help.

During that walk in the woods, Jimmy asked Ruth about her experience. Ruth, in turn, asked Jimmy about his own life, about the depth of his own religious commitment. "Would you be willing," she

Jimmy Carter, beside Rosalynn, Amy, and Miss Lillian, bends his head in silent prayer. (Rafshoon)

The Plains Baptist Church in a quiet moment, without the crowds and banners. The integration issue has become very heated among the membership. Originally, the Plains Baptist Church and the Lebanon Baptist Church had been one—white and black together. However, during Reconstruction, each group, for its own reasons, wanted separation. Healing that rift after a hundred years has been difficult. When the church met to consider expelling the minister for his handling of the desegregation issue, the minister sat alone in a front pew, listening to the harsh words against him. At first, no one spoke up for him. Miss Lillian, whose relationship with the church had been strained for years, knew it was hopeless for her to speak for him. However, she rose from her seat and walked up to sit beside him. Soon after that, Jimmy Carter walked to the front of the church to speak in defense of the minister. When the issue came to a vote, the minister was not expelled, but he later resigned. (Neyland)

Looking down Hudson Street toward the Plains Baptist Church, the church where, until recently, Jimmy Carter was a member and taught Sunday School. (Neyland)

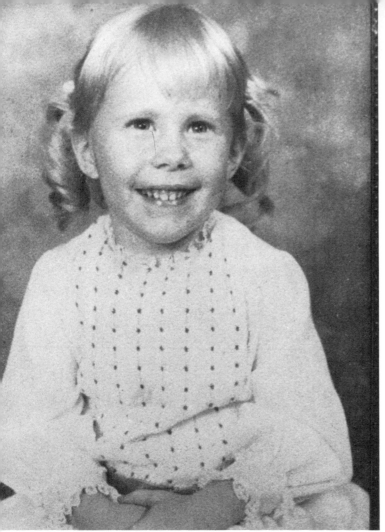

Miss Lillian's favorite photograph of Amy.
(Neyland, courtesy of the Carter family)

---

asked, "to give up everything for Christ? Your life, your possessions?" Jimmy answered affirmatively, but then Ruth asked, "Would you be willing to give up politics?"

This was the crucial question to Jimmy Carter, the question that he could not have asked himself. After much thought, his answer was no. He had to admit that his interest in politics was not just to help others. He liked the prestige and the success. He enjoyed being a leader, and he prided himself on the fact that he alone was responsible for whatever success he had had. He had not yet achieved the complete humility necessary to being "born of the spirit."

Much thought and prayer were necessary before Jimmy could truly humble him-self before God. He and Ruth knelt and prayed that day, and he sought the selflessness that would enable him to turn his life over to a greater power than his own.

The terms that Baptists use to describe this experience make it sound mystical and confuse even many of their own membership. "Do you accept Jesus Christ," they ask, "as your personal Lord and Savior?" To the average person that question sounds silly. In translation, it means, "Will you accept a power higher than yourself to lead you and guide you in every aspect of your life, whether it is what *you* want or not?" Jimmy Carter eventually answered yes. And, when he ran for governor the second time, it was not for himself, nor for his pride and honor. It was for Christ.

Now that term—*Christ*—is probably the most confusing of all the Baptist words.

Miss Lillian's Pond House outside Plains. The original Carter Pond House burned, and the Carter children built this one for their mother while she was away in India. It was a place of quiet companionship for Miss Lillian and Amy during the presidential campaign. After the election, it was taken over temporarily as a guest house for distinguished visitors who came to Plains to plan the new administration. (Neyland)

A photograph of a family gathering at the Pond House soon after Miss Lillian returned from India. Left to right, seated on the steps: Jeff, Miss Lillian, Jimmy, Gloria with Marle, Rosalynn with Amy, Jana (behind), Walter Spann (in front), Buddy, Kim, and Billy. Seated in front: Sybil with Mandy on her lap. Mandy and Amy, who are about the same age, have grown up as close friends. (Neyland, courtesy of the Carter family)

Miss Lillian, Amy, and stuffed animals, outside the Pond House. (Neyland, courtesy of the Carter family)

Christ is looked upon by Baptists as a personal friend. And in a way He is. In a way, He is synonymous with God; but, in another way, He is not.

To attempt to put the simple Baptist faith into more intellectual terms: Jesus Christ was the manifestation of God in man, the extension of the Jewish Yaweh into the daily life and affairs of human beings. Christ always spoke of his message as "the way." The Jews did not have to follow "the way"; they were God's chosen people. But anyone—Jew or Gentile—could choose to be blessed (or chosen) by following the example of Christ in his daily life. It did not mean giving up one's goals or wealth or possessions, but it did mean being willing to do so, if those possessions or goals interfered with one's goodness or humility or obedience.

A great many born-again Baptists understand this, but not in intellectual or theological terminology. Jimmy Carter does not talk like an intellectual, but he has the intelligence to understand, and in his extensive readings, he has included the great theologians Tillich, Niebuhr, and Kierkegaard. Although they don't use the Baptist terminology, and most Baptists would be completely unable to relate to what they say, Jimmy Carter can see that they are all saying essentially the same thing.

In the beginning of *Why Not the Best?*, Jimmy includes a quote from Reinhold Niebuhr: "The sad duty of politics is to establish justice in a sinful world." It was with that attitude that Jimmy returned to politics.

But it must be emphasized that Jimmy Carter is simply a man; he is not to be worshiped. From the time of his "rebirth," Jimmy has earnestly asked for the prayers of the people. But he has also been wary of those who would put too much emphasis on the fact that he is a religious man. He is, by his own admission, serving God. But as a man, he is not infallible, and he will make mistakes.

Jimmy and Ruth are the most deeply religious members of the family, at least in terms of outward expression. "I go to church mostly because of Jimmy and Rosalynn," Miss Lillian offers. "I believe in Christ, and I try to live my life like a good Christian. But, because of disagreements we've had in our church, I would have left years ago if Jimmy and Rosalynn hadn't insisted. Billy and Gloria aren't churchgoers; they haven't gone to church for years, but it isn't because they're not religious. They just can't go along with some of the hypocrisy they see."

That year of "rebirth," 1966, was a significant one for various members of the family. For some years, Jimmy and Rosalynn had wanted to have another child; specifically, they wanted a girl. It had been almost fourteen years since their youngest son, Jeff, had been born. Rosalynn was approaching forty, a difficult age for childbearing, and a doctor had discovered a cyst. However, Rosalynn underwent a simple operation, and she and Jimmy had hope once again.

Amy Lynn Carter was born on October 19, 1967, and it was a joyous occasion for all the Carters. Now, at last, Jimmy and Rosalynn had a healthy, delightful little girl!

It was also wonderful news to Miss Lillian. But she was not home to see her new grandchild. In September of 1966 at the age of sixty-eight, Miss Lillian had joined the Peace Corps. At a time when most men and women think of retiring, she was still thinking of ways she could make her life useful to others.

Miss Lillian's assignment was India, and she was working in the birth control program there. However, after her arrival in India, her independent spirit perceived other areas of concern—most notably the problems of lepers. Miss Lillian managed to get herself assigned to work with a doctor so that she could utilize her nursing experience.

Those two years proved to be the most

Mrs. Coretta King, widow of Martin Luther King, Jr., introduces friends to Jimmy Carter. *(Atlanta Journal-Constitution)*

difficult period of her life, physically as well as emotionally. The hardship and the loss of weight were not as serious to her as the frustration of being one of a small group trying to cope with problems of superhuman proportions.

When she returned to the United States and to Plains, Miss Lillian found a surprise awaiting her. Naturally, the family met her at the airport to drive her home to the comfortable brick home on Church Street. But along the roadside were signs proclaiming: "This is the way to Miss Lillian's house." When they arrived in Plains, there were banners and signs in her frontyard saying, "This is Miss Lillian's house" and "Welcome home, Miss Lillian."

There was a party of family and friends to greet her, and it was a tearful and joyful reunion. But, in the midst of the celebration, her children told her they had to take her somewhere "special." So they got back into the cars and set off along the roads. Again there were signs, which Miss Lillian couldn't quite understand. They said: "This is the way to Miss Lillian's Pond House." But the Pond House had burned some years ago.

The signs directed the cars along the road to Archery, and into the left turn that was the familiar red-dirt road to the Pond House. And when the cars stopped at the site, there was another big banner: "This is Miss Lillian's Pond House." And there was

Jimmy Carter is sworn in as governor of the state of Georgia. *(Atlanta Journal-Constitution)*

indeed a beautiful new house nestled among the loblolly pines. Her children had rebuilt her retreat as a special surprise to welcome their mother home.

The house was clean and simple in design, with big glass sliding doors overlooking the pond. It was a private place where she could be alone to walk and think and relax and fish. It was the most wonderful welcome-home present possible—or maybe the second most wonderful.

There was also Amy. And the Pond House was not destined to be just "Miss Lillian's Pond House" but rather "Miss Lillian's and Amy's Pond House." Miss Lillian loved all her grandchildren, but Kim, Billy's oldest, had been her special grandchild. With her return from India, Amy became the special one, and they spent hours, days, and nights together at the Pond House. Swings were installed for Amy, and a hammock for Miss Lillian—but the hammock quickly became Amy's favorite place too.

By the time Miss Lillian had returned from India, Jimmy's campaign for governor was well under way. He had begun that second campaign almost immediately after his first defeat.

Oddly enough, Jimmy's second campaign for governor in 1970 has come in for the most criticism. It was during this time that his behavior seemed least "Christian." Jimmy has never tried to explain or defend what seems to some analysts to be standard political doubletalk. But what occurred, in effect, was that there were *two* sets of issues, and there have been *two* sets of issues in Jimmy Carter's campaigning ever since 1966. There is the one set—narrow, defined, and confined—proscribed by the press and the established special interest groups. It involves very specific questions permitting only a yes or a no, an either or an or. The answers to those specific questions permit very simplistic minds to pigeonhole a candidate. Then there is Jimmy Carter's set of issues—in a mold unfamiliar to the press and the political establishment. These are the issues of the people, that forgotten segment of an over-segmented society.

In 1970, the people were beginning to get tired of candidates who promised this to one group of people, and that to another; they wanted a candidate who intended to act for *all* the people.

The press and the liberal organizations knew what former Governor Carl Sanders was all about; they could pigeonhole him, and so they gave him their support. Having been pigeonholed in the 1966 race as a representative of only the black segment of the population, Jimmy refused in 1970 to be pinned down on questions of desegregation. As a result, the press created a right-wing, racist, "redneck" image for Jimmy Carter. But Jimmy would not be drawn into that sort of defensive, divisive campaign. In his newfound serenity and humility, he pursued his own set of concerns: improvements in education, protection of the environment, a program for mental health, and a reorganization and reform of the state government. These were issues of long-range importance, problems whose solutions were essential to the accomplishment of the specific concerns of the various groups.

His opposition could not understand what he was up to; it was not the kind of simple offensive-defensive campaigning to which they were accustomed. And, when Carl Sanders suddenly found himself on the defensive, he did not even realize what

it was he was defending. When he tried to turn himself from slick city boy to folksy country hero, he thought the issues were still his issues.

Jimmy Carter worked hard to win that election. He worked for four long years; and Rosalynn worked; the rest of his family and his young enthusiastic staff worked.

Rosalynn and Jimmy arriving at the inaugural ball in Atlanta. Rosalynn wore the dress again six years later at the presidential inauguration balls in Washington—not because of frugality, though the Carters are frugal, but because of sentiment. (Atlanta Journal-Constitution)

Jimmy and Rosalynn dancing the first dance at the governor's inaugural ball. Rosalynn's dress hasn't changed, but the hairstyle has. (Wide World)

But Jimmy Carter did not win that election; the people did. And the first ones to be surprised by his actions as governor were the members of the opposition.

Under Jimmy Carter's governship, organizations were set up to ease the racial strife that often accompanied desegregation—organizations in which whites and blacks worked together with common

Governor Jimmy Carter talks to the press after returning from South America, where he discussed establishing trade relations with the state of Georgia. *(Atlanta Journal-Constitution)*

Governor Jimmy Carter and college students run from Athens, Georgia, to Atlanta to raise money for the March of Dimes in 1974. *(Atlanta Journal-Constitution)*

Mental health became the concern of Rosalynn Carter as first lady of Georgia, and the olympics for retarded children were a special project. *(Atlanta Journal-Constitution)*

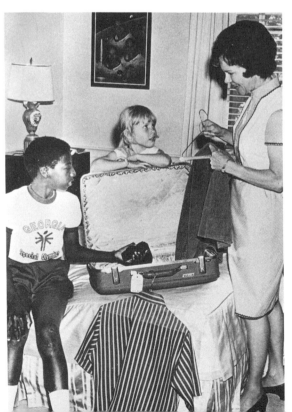

purpose and concern. Great strides were made in the criminal justice system, and in the prisons (where most of the inmates were black) by incorporating new educational programs to alleviate recidivism. Black leaders were appointed to important boards and committees overseeing education, law enforcement, the penal system, and the licensing of doctors, dentists, nurses, barbers, and hairdressers. And, for the first time, portraits of important black Georgians—Martin Luther King, Jr., Lucy Laney, and Henry MacNeal Turner—were hung along with those of the whites in the state capitol.

One of Jimmy's major concerns as governor was conservation of natural resources. He made numerous trips to inspect waterways and sites of intended projects by the Army Corps of Engineers. (Neyland, courtesy of the Carter family)

As an incentive to business and commerce, Jimmy and Rosalynn journeyed to South America to try to establish trade relations. Consular offices were set up in Atlanta for numerous European, Asian, and South American countries, as the state widened its economic scope to include the world. And a World Trade Center was built in Atlanta.

But perhaps the most significant accomplishment of Jimmy's term as governor

was his reorganization of the state bureaucracy. He instituted what he called "zero-based budgeting," which meant that each department and each program would be reevaluated annually to determine whether there was still a need for the moneys allocated and spent. Various departments were consolidated to avoid duplication and waste; when before there might have been twenty-two agencies governing water resources, there would now be one. In the welfare department, the number of caseworkers on a welfare case was often reduced from seven to two. In the law enforcement sector, state troopers who had been trained and outfitted at great public expense, were found to be typing, filing, and answering telephones;

Jimmy Carter's proudest moment as governor of Georgia—signing into law his government reorganization bill. (Atlanta Journal-Constitution)

As the daughter of a governor, of a candidate for president, and of a president, Amy Carter has not lost out on any of the normal benefits of childhood. Here, she goes trick-or-treating accompanied by her father. *(Atlanta Journal-Constitution)*

Jimmy's government reassigned them to patrol duty and put trained handicapped citizens into offices to man phones and typewriters.

When Jimmy Carter entered office, there were three hundred separate state agencies; by the time he left office, he had uncovered the fact that 278 of them were either totally unnecessary or were duplicating the work of others. In actual dollars and cents, it is difficult to imagine what the savings were to the state of Georgia. Critics who slyly total up expenditures during the

four years Jimmy was actually in office don't recognize that fiscal years don't match precisely with terms of office, and they do not include the effects of inflation. Perhaps the fair estimate for the four years, taking inflation into account, is that he saved the Georgia taxpayers $116,000,000 without depriving them of a single important service, and without depriving any tenured government employees of their jobs.

But Jimmy Carter was not the only member of the family serving the public. Jimmy had asked Rosalynn to take on the important matter of mental health. Having already faced up to touring the state, meeting people, speaking, and campaigning, the quiet, shy wife was again faced with a challenge. Rosalynn took to working with retarded and emotionally disturbed patients—particularly children. Her soft-spoken, sweet manner was comforting, and she quickly established a rapport with them. But public speaking was something else. Her first speech before the Georgia State Mental Health Association was a long one, which she memorized. But she was in absolute terror the whole evening that she might stumble or somehow make a complete fool of herself. Soon after, however, with Jimmy's guidance, Rosalynn learned to extemporize, and she began to warm up to the task of public speaking.

Serving as hostess at the Governor's Mansion was also a challenge. The personages she had to entertain were prestigious, sophisticated government leaders from all over the world. And Rosalynn had to learn to handle and plan complicated seating arrangements and a wide variety of menus.

Amy was three when her family moved into the Governor's Mansion in Atlanta, and she was seven when they moved out. Her bright, playful personality gave Jimmy's governorship a warm and human tone. She was intelligent, perceptive, and sometimes mischievous, lightening a time that might have been otherwise overburdened.

The other Carter children were either already adults or almost grown-up, and they were beginning lives of their own. Jack was married in 1971 to Juliette Langford; and Chip followed two years later, marrying Caron Griffin. Jeff, aged eighteen when his father was elected governor, was in college. So Amy became the darling of the public and the delight of photographers.

When his four successful years as governor were concluded, Jimmy's decision about the next step was almost automatic. When Miss Lillian asked what he intended to do, Jimmy responded somewhat wryly, "I guess I'll have to run for president."

"President of what?" inquired Miss Lillian.

But the decision was not quite *that* lightly made. It was a serious decision, and he did give the campaign careful thought. In fact, Jimmy had been thinking about running for the presidency ever since the 1972 presidential campaign. As governor of the state of Georgia, he had come to know a great many of the presidential aspirants, and he had also come to realize that he was as qualified as any of them for the office. The problem was that the people didn't know that. Not yet.

Jimmy Carter may have shown enterprise by selling peanuts as a youngster, but his daughter Amy is no slouch herself. During her father's presidential race, she opened a stand in front of their house, selling lemonade first at five cents a glass, later at ten cents, and finally at a quarter before the Secret Service blockade put her out of business. This photo was taken after Amy and her father had been discussing a new idea of Amy's—charging the photographers ten cents for each photo they took of her. Before Jimmy could tell the photographers her plan, Amy silenced him by clapping her hand over his mouth. (UPI)

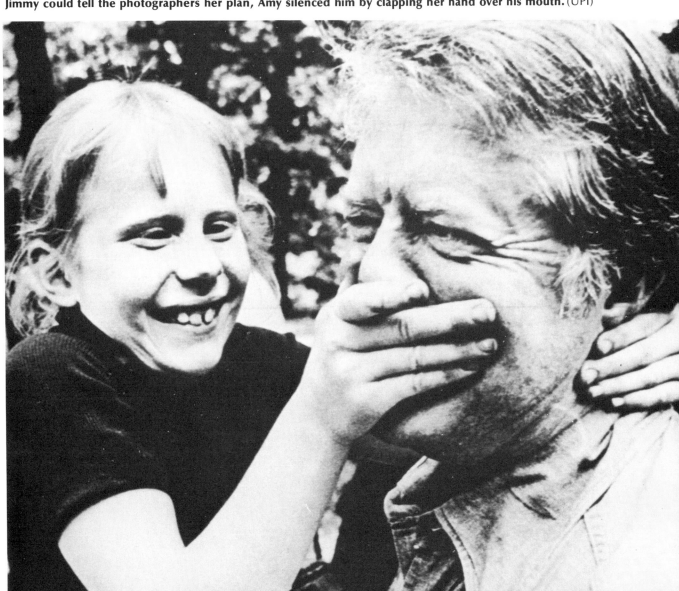

Risen Again

"Save your Confederate money, boys," Southerners used to say, "the South's gonna rise again!" It was usually said half in jest. Nobody ever really believed the Confederacy would pull away from the Union a second time; but most Southerners never did accept the total domination imposed on them by the North, a domination that lasted much longer than the nation's domination of foreign enemies in other wars.

Even today, Northerners visit the South, look about them, and comment, "This is another country entirely." The South is not quite that, but it has defiantly held on to its own culture and its own social patterns for over a century.

And, at long last, the South has risen again. It has done so in a way that the South never expected—it has rejoined the Union by choice. After two decades of inner turmoil over desegregation, South-

erners, black and white, are working out their problems of guilt and retribution far more successfully than their Northern counterparts; they can now stand beside their Yankee brothers and say with dignity, "We have something to offer you." The wounds of five generations can be healed.

Oddly enough, the great democrats, the great believers in human rights before the Civil War, were Southerners—George Washington, Thomas Jefferson, James Madison, James Monroe, Andrew Jackson, Henry Clay, John Calhoun, John Randolph. They were most of them commoners, or at the very least, believers in the common man. The fact that some of them did not consider black Africans to be men was a very serious flaw, but the great virtue of the South is that the belief in the common man has persisted longer than the belief that blacks are not human.

James Earl Carter, Jr. is representative of the best that the South has to offer. He is a common man, and he is a strong believer in human rights, very much in the tradition of the great democrats. He believes in the

---

The Jimmy grin on the Great Pumpkin. Some laughed, but Jimmy kept smiling. (Wide World)

people—all of the people, whatever their color—and he believes that a president must remain close to the people because he is their servant.

When Jimmy Carter decided to run for the presidency, he knew there was only one way for him to do it: to take his candidacy to the people. In that respect, the 1975–76 election was a perfect meeting of candidate and system. By 1975, the use of presidential preference primaries—rather than the old "smoke-filled room" process—had come to be the only way of selecting party candidates. The voters in the various states, and not the political party bosses, selected the man for whom their delegates would vote in the party conventions.

Since the very beginning of Jimmy's political career, he had opposed individuals or groups who attempted to keep the power away from the people. Although he knew that he would eventually have to gain the support of powerful individuals and groups, he also realized he would not have to be obligated to those individuals and groups if he first had the support of the people. For that reason, the primary system seemed to be made for his kind of politics.

Jimmy Carter began his campaign in January of 1975 in Iowa, a state that has a party caucus rather than a presidential preference primary. Despite that slight difference, Jimmy was able to take his candidacy to the people. In fact, he found he *had* to go to the people. For his first reception in Des Moines, only three people showed up. So he and his family and his campaign workers hit the streets, introducing themselves, extending their hands, and explaining personally what they were about. They went from door to door; if people weren't at home, the Carters wrote personal notes.

Unlike traditional political candidates, Jimmy Carter was treating people like people; he was meeting them as one human being to another. The professional politicians and the veteran newsmen scorned him, finding him difficult to pin down on their issues. But, as before in Georgia, Jimmy Carter's issues were not the issues of professional politicians and newsmen. The people understood; they lived Jimmy Carter's issues each day; the other issues they simply read about in the newspapers.

Jimmy didn't take a majority of the delegates in Iowa, but he took more than any other candidate. And, with the help of the people of Georgia—the Peanut Brigade—he went on from there to take New Hampshire.

In the bitter cold of January and February of 1975, an airliner full of people from Jimmy's home state arrived in New Hampshire. They walked the Northern streets telling the people what kind of a man Jimmy Carter is. It was a "people-to-people" campaign, Rebs speaking to Yankees, finding much in common, and talking about a common man for president. By primary day in New Hampshire, February 24, Jimmy was out in front, ahead of the other more experienced candidates for the Democratic nomination.

But surprisingly, Jimmy lost in the March 2 primary in the populist state of Massachusetts, coming in a sad fourth. A week later, however, he was back on top with the Florida primary.

As Jimmy attracted more and more attention, questions about his religious beliefs began to come up in meetings and in the press. Jimmy is an avowed Southern Baptist; and he actually practices his religion, doesn't just give lip-service to it. Could this affect the separation of church and state? Some people worried. Sure, the country had elected a Roman Catholic in 1960—but this was different, this was a Southern Baptist! And as far as most liberals and intellectuals knew, the Southern Baptist faith was about as rigid a religion as there could be. It was, they thought, synonymous with the Ku Klux Klan, lynchings, and Jew-baiting. They had a lot to learn.

Oddly, most people have a tendency to assume that those of other backgrounds are totally unlike themselves—possibly even the antithesis of themselves. Assumptions make for prejudices, and unfortunately, everybody makes assumptions, even liberal intellectuals. But as people got to know Jimmy Carter, their prejudices against Southern Baptists began to erode.

Jimmy judged rightly that the only way to get over people's concern about his religion was to talk about it. That decision created a few extra headaches, a few myths and misconceptions.

Jimmy Carter fears neither hard work nor making himself appear ludicrous. During the campaign for the Democratic presidential nomination, he took time out to drain the pond at the Pond House, getting in up to his neck. (UPI)

Because the pond is manmade rather than natural, cleaning it is necessary to maintain a proper balance of fish and plant life. Here a muddy Jimmy Carter can be seen rescuing a few fish in a net. (Atlanta Journal-Constitution)

Amy Carter helped out in the cleaning of the pond, taking an opportunity rare in the life of a child—playing in the mud with parental approval. (Atlanta Journal-Constitution)

Jimmy chose to discuss the subject first in a Southern state, in a speaking engagement in Winston-Salem, North Carolina. "I don't think I'm ordained by God to be president," he assured his listeners, and then went on to explain that his religion is

a personal one and that it would not place limitations upon his duties as president. It was at a press conference the next day that he described his "born again" experience with his sister Ruth. He tried to explain that it was simply a spiritual adjustment he had had to make, and not a mystical experience. However, his listeners couldn't quite see the fine distinction.

Jimmy displays his catch. (Wide World)

On the campaign trail, Jimmy Carter participates in a Democratic tug of war in California. Senator John Tunney is the man in the plaid shirt. (Wide World)

Jimmy meant it when he asked his supporters to pray for him, just as he has meant it when he has asked the people for their help. In all humility, he knows that he is simply one person and that he needs as much guidance and assistance as any human being.

Jimmy helps to clean and scale the fish for a fish fry and barbecue behind Billy's service station. (Atlanta Journal-Constitution)

With brother Billy, Jimmy digs into some of the food at the fish fry and barbecue. (Wide World)

Jimmy's direct and honest profession of his religion has had other effects, some of them good, some bad, some of them hard to judge. He did get the prayers of the people; thousands of them of all religious backgrounds wrote to him from all over the country to tell him they were remembering him in their prayers. Later, after the election, Jimmy remembered these people above all others, sending each and every one of them an invitation to his inauguration. (He even sent one to a woman sentenced to life in prison in Huntsville, Texas, for killing her husband.)

But strong religious beliefs also attract fanatics and the mentally unbalanced, and sometimes it was difficult to distinguish between the truly good and religious people and the lunatic fringe, who wanted to harangue Jimmy and to convert him to their way of thinking.

People of various religious persuasions flocked to Plains to try to convey their own religious messages to the candidate. Some came to proselytize with banners and signs, some simply to attract publicity. On Sundays they gathered in front of the Plains Baptist Church, giving the religious services something of a carnival atmosphere, reminiscent to some of the moneychangers in the temple. They passed out their religious tracts and bent the ears of anyone who would listen. Some simply admonished the listeners to pray. Some lectured on the evils of racial integration. And some warned of Armageddon.

There was also the Rev. Clennon King, who appeared each Sunday to try to join the church. Most Sundays he would be invited inside to worship, but he refused to enter unless he entered as a member. He would stay outside the church long enough to have his picture taken and then leave. In the beginning, the newsmen and the people of Plains took him seriously, but after he consistently refused to enter to worship and to get to know the other church members, they began to ignore him.

Jimmy Carter doesn't get much time to play ball these days, and when he does it's usually with newsmen on the diamond at Plains High School. (UPI)

One of the most unusual stories to come out of the campaign involves a man from Israel, a truly religious man whom many consider to be a genuine prophet of God. Aaron Levy is Jewish, but he has been associated with an establishment of the Baptists in Israel known as Bethel Zion. Early in the campaign, long before Jimmy Carter became known internationally, Aaron Levy began to have dreams and visions concerning the candidate. God was commanding Aaron Levy to go to the United States to anoint Jimmy Carter with oil and to convey His blessings upon him. This had to be accomplished before the election, before Carter assumed the presidency.

It took Rosalynn Carter a while to adjust to introducing herself to people; but as strangers warmed up to her, she began to enjoy campaigning. Jimmy has relied on her opinions often, and she has proved to be an excellent judge of the political scene. (Wide World)

A few days before the election, however, Jimmy did visit Dallas, and by what can only be described as a miraculous set of circumstances, Aaron Levy managed to get through the Secret Service to see the candidate.

Levy is small in stature, and he speaks little English, relying on his wife to translate for him. Though Jimmy's first reaction must surely have been wariness, he chose to hear what Levy had to say. In his broken English, Levy explained his dreams and visions and told Jimmy that God had sent him to convey His blessing. Jimmy accepted the anointing with oil and knelt while Levy prayed in Hebrew.

Because of the language difficulties, Jimmy did not know precisely what was happening. But for Aaron Levy that was not the important factor. What was important was that he had accomplished his task before the election, and he was able to return to Israel.

The story never appeared in the newspapers, but it has been discussed widely among what is known as the "charismatic movement" within the Baptist Church. The

The Reverend Clennon King talks to admirers and poses for photographs after refusing to worship at the Plains Baptist Church. (Neyland)

Levy had limited finances, and he had no idea of how he would find Carter, or even if Carter would see him. He did, however, have contacts with the Beverly Hills Baptist Church in Dallas, Texas. He used what money he had, traveled to Dallas, and waited for God to bring Jimmy Carter to him.

Aaron Levy waited for a long time. When Rosalynn Carter traveled through Dallas, making a brief appearance there, Levy managed to speak to her. Rosalynn thanked him graciously for his prayers but explained that it was not likely that Jimmy would be coming to Dallas.

Miss Lillian takes pride in having introduced Andrew Young to Jimmy. Young, now the Ambassador to the United Nations, is seen here with his son Andrew III. (UPI)

meaning of the anointing is not precisely clear, although it did have the effect of changing the votes of a great many members of the Beverly Hills Baptist Church in Dallas, Texas—most of them Republicans—after Aaron Levy spoke to them in the Bronco Bowl.

Jimmy Carter has tried to keep his religion in proper perspective ever since it became an issue. Though some believe him to be ordained by God to lead the country and the world out of a difficult time, Jimmy himself has no such pretensions. He sees himself as simply a man, subject to the same failings as any other man. He does believe in God, and he tries earnestly to do God's will, but he does not consider himself to have any special favor or dispensation.

In Winston-Salem, North Carolina, he said: "I don't think God is going to make me president, by any means; but whatever I have as a responsibility for the rest of my life, it will be with that intimate, personal continuing relationship with God, through Christ, that has given me peace."

In the long run, the religious issue did not hurt Jimmy's campaign. Jimmy won a resounding victory in the North Carolina primary on March 23. If it hurt him anywhere, it hurt him in New York, on April 6, where he suffered his second primary defeat. However, that same day, Jimmy won in Wisconsin, so he still held on to his slight lead.

But soon, another non-issue was to be turned into an issue by the press, which still could not look upon this provincial Southerner as a serious contender for the presidency. One reporter pounced upon a chance phrase that Jimmy had used in a minor interview—that phrase was *ethnic purity*. To simplistic liberal minds, that could mean only one thing: racial segregation; and the reporters and newscasters had a field day.

But the people—black and white, Jewish and Gentile, Irish, Italian, Czech, and Polish—knew very well what he meant.

After Jimmy received the nomination of his party, he no longer had to seek out the people; they sought him. (Wide World)

When the subject came up on television, they simply groaned, changed the channel, and voted the way they wanted to vote. After all, a Jewish mother doesn't want her daughter to marry a goy; a good Jewish boy would be preferable. And a black family doesn't seek to buy a nice house because they want white neighbors; they just want to buy a nice house, wherever it happens to be.

"Ethnic purity" became the issue of the press and Jimmy's opposition in the Pennsylvania primary, but Jimmy and the people won on primary day. And Jimmy's good friend, Andrew Young, a black congressman from Georgia, helped the campaign past that unfortunate phrase.

Whether it was the "ethnic purity" slip, or their own ingrained prejudice against Southerners, the liberal establishment of the Democratic Party decided that they had to do something to stop what was beginning to look like a Carter landslide. Carter had already beaten each of the other candidates in one state or another, so new candidates entered the race in Texas, Nebraska, Maryland, Michigan, Oregon, Rhode Island, Idaho, Nevada, South Dakota, California, New Jersey, and Ohio.

In the first few states, the new candidates did cut into Jimmy's edge, but not very seriously. With his resounding victory in Ohio on June 8, after winning in Texas, Michigan, Tennessee, Kentucky, Arkansas, and South Dakota, Jimmy Carter just about had the nomination sewn up.

But he hadn't done it alone. His family had been out stumping as much as he had, and a great many of the voters were casting their ballots as much for Rosalynn and Miss Lillian and Ruth and Gloria and Billy as for Jimmy Carter.

Rosalynn had been meeting the challenge of politicking—meeting the people, answering the questions of the press, giving impromptu speeches—as well as or better than political wives who had been in the game for years. She still got butterflies in her stomach, and it continued to be an

Amy Carter and her father delight in a bit of nature study—a pet hamster named Sleepy in its maze. (Wide World)

tory in the limited time. In the early days, Rosalynn had to push herself onto people and into situations where she could get attention. In the later weeks, she had become recognizable to the public, and they flocked to her enthusiastically. As the Democratic convention approached, she actually began to enjoy herself.

Rosalynn reads avidly, as do all the other Carters. Rosalynn prefers history and historical fiction; Jimmy usually reads economics; Miss Lillian loves a good mystery, and Amy prefers Nancy Drew. Here, Rosalynn carries The President's Mistress, **by Patrick Anderson.**
(Wide World)

effort for her to break through her natural reserve. But these factors worked to her advantage: each time she met someone, each time she answered a question, each time she spoke in public, it was with a freshness and a genuineness that made people listen.

Here was a woman to respect and admire. After years of public women who came off either as plastic, hypocritical, sexless, bored, or downright exploitative, it was refreshing to both men and women to meet a campaign wife who was the genuine article—a woman who was both attractive and independent. Whenever the subject of Rosalynn came up—whether it was in New York or California, Texas or Minnesota—someone was bound to say, "By God, you've got to admire a woman like that."

The campaign was tiring and difficult for Rosalynn—she had to go for weeks at a time without seeing Jimmy or Amy. She and Jimmy had decided it would be better to move about the country separately, so that they could cover twice as much terri-

The public enthusiasm for Rosalynn Carter should not be counted lightly. At a time when there have been confusion, uncertainty, and an overabundance of talk combined with an underabundance of action about the changing role of women, there is an unspoken message in the actions of

Rosalynn Carter. She is an example of what an independent woman, a wife, and mother, can be. She has not arrived at that point alone; it has been the result of both her own energies and the sympathetic pride and encouragement of her loving husband. Rosalynn Carter could not have been what she is without Jimmy; and Jimmy Carter could not have been what he is without Rosalynn; and neither could have done it without love.

If credit is to be given where credit is due, it is necessary to point to other loving relationships. Jimmy's attitude toward Rosalynn could not have existed if it hadn't been for the example of Miss Lillian and Mr. Earl. Now, a lot of people try to make out that there is hostility between Miss Lillian and Rosalynn; they can't see how two strong and independent women can possibly be related to one man. But there is nothing but respect, admiration, and love between Jimmy's wife and his mother. In a way, the independent Rosalynn Carter could not have existed if it had not been for the independent Lillian Carter; and the independent Lillian Carter could not have existed if it had not been for the attitude of Earl Carter.

Maybe the drift is beginning to become clear: there yet remains some significance to the institution of the American family. There is yet some meaning to love, as old-fashioned as that may seem.

Gloria and Ruth didn't take anything away from themselves or their families by going out and campaigning for their brother; Miss Lillian didn't take anything away from herself by looking after Amy while Jimmy and Rosalynn were traveling about the country. And Amy hasn't missed out on any love by spending time with her grandmother at the Pond House; if anything, she has gained.

Amy herself, without even knowing it, helped get the Carter message across, helped bring in the votes. Amy is her own person; she is respectful and polite, but she is also independent. Her lemonade stand became famous, and people laughed affectionately at her jousts with reporters. But when she became testy, the people also got her message: sure, I'm a public figure, and I'll give you some time, but only so much; the rest of my time is my own.

The other Carter children—Jack, Chip, and Jeff—said essentially the same thing, though perhaps not so simply or directly as Amy. Jack, the oldest, with a wife and son, campaigned for his father, but kept his own life and career quite private. Of the three sons, Jack is the serious one, the most studious. Chip is the most politically oriented, and he threw himself wholeheartedly into the campaign. Jeff, the youngest son, was married in 1975, early in the campaign, and continued to work for his father while setting quietly about his own life.

Of the sons, Chip is the most likely to follow his father into politics. He is outgoing, personable, and filled with energy. But, as a reflection of the loving family relationship, Jeff is perhaps the most interesting. Jeff has the same interest in nature and in Indian artifacts and lore that his father has. (Jimmy's hobby is collecting arrowheads and Indian pottery, and he is known as an authority on Georgia tribes.) And Jeff is easygoing and friendly, not shy so much as quiet and unassuming. As a small child, he was accident prone; and every time he fell, he seemed to land on his face, breaking bones or cartilage. On the advice of doctors, Jimmy and Rosalynn decided to wait until he was older to correct the damage. To another child, this problem and the extensive corrective surgery might have been a handicap. But, largely because of his loving family relationship, Jeff has grown up as secure and normal as any other child. It is love that heals wounds as much as it is medical attention. And healing is what all of the Carters are about—whether it is Miss Lillian tending to the sick in Sumter County or in India; or Ruth Carter Stapleton touring the country lecturing about inner spiritual healing through Christ's love; or Jimmy Carter pardoning draft evaders and inviting them home from exile.

When the Democratic Party met in Madison Square Garden in New York, healing was the theme of the convention. Jimmy went into the convention with the nomination pretty much sewn up, and he turned his energies toward bringing all the various groups together. After all the talk about "ethnic purity," blacks and whites were together at the convention, and they sang "We Shall Overcome," a song that could not have been sung at any convention twenty or even twelve years ago. It was a moving moment, and so was the speech by Barbara Jordan, a black congresswoman from Texas. And so was the closing benediction given by the Rev. Martin Luther King, Sr.

Jimmy's selection of a vice presidential running mate was probably the best possible one—Walter F. Mondale, a hardworking liberal senator from Minnesota. The choice was a confirmation of Jimmy's own progressive views, as well as a gesture of reconciliation toward those liberals who had doggedly refused to believe in him.

Jimmy's acceptance speech emphasized love and healing; it was a positive speech, one that spoke of what he and his party could do together, and not one that attempted to attack or demean their opposition. And, in closing, he referred to the listeners as his "bothers and sisters," a phrase that harkened back to his Southern Baptist religion, but one that also joined his party into the fold as part of his family. He was offering his love and asking for his party's love in return.

To convey his meaning by actions as well as words, he called upon other party leaders—some of whom had opposed him—to join him on the podium: Governor Milton Schapp, Senator Edmund Muskie, Senator Hubert Humphrey, Governor Edmund Brown, Governor Wendell Anderson, Senator Frank Church, Representative Barbara Jordan, Sargent Shriver. It was a

The love and closeness between Jimmy and Rosalynn Carter have grown with the years. Jimmy has no self-consciousness about displaying his love in public. Here, he is seen kissing Rosalynn after completing his acceptance speech at the Democratic convention. (Wide World)

dramatic moment.

The Party did heal its wounds; it did unify and work together for the election of Jimmy Carter. Compared to his race for the nomination, the race for his election against the Republican incumbent was relatively quiet. Jimmy continued to campaign person to person, and that continued to be the way he best conveyed his

85

Jimmy and grandson Jason watch the Democratic convention on television from Jimmy's New York hotel room. (Wide World)

Rosalynn and Jimmy Carter, Walter and Joan Mondale accept the ovations at Madison Square Garden at the close of the convention. (Wide World)

An emotional moment near the close of the Democratic convention. Jimmy and Miss Lillian embrace, while Rosalynn and Amy look out over the cheering crowds. (Wide World)

The Carters bow their heads while the Reverend Martin Luther King, Sr. delivers the benediction on closing night at Madison Square Garden. (Wide World)

Speaking in front of large crowds once terrified Rosalynn; now she delights in the challenge. Here, she rehearses with Leonard Bernstein at Constitution Hall in Washington for a performance of Aaron Copland's A Lincoln Portrait. (Wide World)

Jimmy Carter's decision to walk from the Capitol to the White House was unprecedented in American history. The implications of the act in this era are limitless: most basically, it shows that he considers himself a common man; perhaps more significantly, it shows that he trusts—and does not fear—the American people. (Neyland)

message. But running as the official Democratic candidate was just a bit different from running for the candidacy: Jimmy couldn't meet *all* the people face to face. He had to reach some of the people by way of television, and through debating his opponent in the first televised debates since 1960.

Debating wasn't exactly Jimmy's way, because he was forced to emphasize the differences between people rather than their similarities, but he acquitted himself well—at least as well as his opponent, and his opponent was the incumbent President.

Much of the opposition's attacks were simply superficial needling—like joking about his smile and talking about country singers and grits in the White House; and straining to prove that Jimmy could tell a lie by juggling the Georgia budgets to

make it appear that he hadn't actually saved the state any money.

But most of the people saw through these to the more important issues; most understood what Jimmy was trying to say, even though many were almost afraid to hope that he meant what he said. And, on election day, Jimmy won—not by enough to inflate his ego, but by enough to make him president.

And he won through a coalition of those old Democratic stand-bys, the industrial North and the agrarian South. The coalition may have been old, but the constituency wasn't: it was a new North and a new South. It was a South that had enfranchised the black voters, and a North where racial relations were strained. Together, they elected a Southerner president, a Southerner who promised to heal their wounds.

Celebration

Jimmy Carter's return to Plains as the newly elected President was a joyous occasion. The community-family of Jimmy's hometown came out to welcome him and to celebrate in full force. The celebration continued through Thanksgiving and Christmas and the inauguration. And it hasn't stopped yet. Plains is justifiably proud of its man and of his miraculous rise to the most important office in the land.

December 1976, between the election and the inauguration, was a wonderful time in the small Georgia town. Christmas spirit mixed with election joy, creating an abundance of goodwill.

Even Billy Carter's defeat when he ran for mayor of Plains didn't dampen the good spirits. Billy himself accepted the results good-naturedly. With cousin Hugh in the Georgia legislature and Jimmy in the White House, a Carter as mayor might be one too many in public office.

Of course, despite the celebrations, there were differences of opinion in Plains, as there are in any community, but the people of Plains don't permit those differences to separate them in any serious way. A good example is the case of the Christmas tree.

Traditionally, Plains had always transplanted a beautiful live tree into the park along Main Street for the Christmas season, and then returned it to its natural surroundings when Christmas was over. After Jimmy's election, with the eyes of the world focused on the town, a minor dispute arose over the practice. One faction wanted to continue the tradition; the other wanted to do things the fancy way and buy an expensive plastic tree and plastic ornaments for the street lights.

The plastic-tree faction won, and they bought the best that money could buy. But even after the tree was installed, complete with blinking lights, the natural-tree faction, led by Billy Carter, continued to grumble silently.

One night, when most of the town was asleep, a tow truck appeared in the park and took most of the plastic tree with it,

It was a tearful moment that Wednesday after the election, when Jimmy and Rosalynn returned to Plains to be greeted by proud and jubilant neighbors. (Wide World)

dropping branches along the way to Americus, Georgia, and leaving only a small portion of the tree still blinking in the park.

Many people blamed Billy Carter, who earnestly denied any wrongdoing, and there were those who supported him, saying with knowing smiles, "I know who it was, and it wasn't Billy."

Meanwhile, the town was temporarily treeless. But after a few days, with no fanfare, a new tree—a natural cedar—appeared in front of Billy Carter's service station. The tree had a beer can on top.

Soon after that, a bulldozer with a lift was brought, and Billy's daughter Jana and some of the "good ol' boys" climbed up to decorate the tree.

It is not that the Carter family objects to plastic, when it's used for practical purposes. They just prefer live vegetation. Privately Miss Lillian confesses, "I detest plastic flowers; I'm allergic to them." But she graciously accepts plastic flower arrangements when they are given to her.

Differences of opinion are an important part of what this country is all about—whether they concern Christmas trees, plastic flowers, or the construction of a new nuclear bomber. This is something that Jimmy Carter understands.

Meeting Jimmy Carter and his family—in the midst of the Christmas celebration—vindicated my vote for him. And the time I spent with Miss Lillian was further evidence of the remarkable qualities of the new First Family. We sat for several days in the depot, as she doggedly greeted and thanked the public, despite the increasing pain in her arms and legs. It was a great strain, meeting people day after day—especially draining because she endeavored to express a personal interest in each one. By her manner, she seemed to be saying: Our people deserve respect from their leaders and from their leaders' families.

The more I got to know Miss Lillian, the more I came to like and respect her. Despite all the public attention, she was determined to continue to live as an ordinary person. She continued to cook her own meals, ran her own errands, and did her own shopping. Between appearances at the depot and charity telethons, she tried to find time to do her Christmas shopping and to have a quiet dinner at home with Jimmy. And Jimmy, too, looked forward to the simple dinner of steak, potatoes, and ambrosia, and a chance to sit quietly and talk, out of the limelight.

The day after her dinner with Jimmy, Miss Lillian asked me to come by to meet her daughter Gloria and to help her put up her own Christmas tree. However, it turned out that she was too tired to "fool with the tree," so we sat and talked.

I had been a bit apprehensive about meeting Gloria. As far as I or the general public knew, she was simply "a motorcycle nut." I expected her to show up in jeans, motorcycle boots, and a leather jacket. But she was not at all as I expected. Although she possesses that inner strength that is so typical of the Carters, she looks like anybody else in a small town. As I got to know her better, I learned that she is also sensi-

tive, very literate, politically astute, and uncannily wise.

I ran into Gloria on the street the next morning, on my way over to set up the Christmas tree. "Mother's in the hospital," she informed me. "She's not supposed to have any visitors, but she wants to see you." Miss Lillian's illness did not seem to

On Wednesday, after the presidential election returns came in with Jimmy Carter the winner, Miss Lillian displayed a green T-shirt with the words "Jimmy Won! 76." (Wide World)

For emergency reading, Miss Lillian resorts to a folding lorgnette, a gift from Jimmy. But she can't quite manage the prim demeanor to go with it. (Neyland)

After the election, the Carters spent some time on St. Simon's Island, off the coast of Georgia, to relax and make plans for the transition to the White House. This time, Jimmy didn't carry his luggage off the airplane, but did help with the file boxes. *(Atlanta Constitution-Journal, Calvin Cruce)*

Billy Carter relaxes with some of the good ol' boys in his service station. (Neyland)

Billy Carter watches one of his friends demonstrate a birdlike puppet that his daughter made. (Neyland)

Jana Carter, lifted up by a bulldozer, begins decorating the Christmas tree in front of her father's service station. Jana did not place the beer can at the top. (Neyland)

Vice President Mondale leaves the railroad depot after greeting some of the visitors to Plains. (Neyland)

Vice President Mondale's motorcade leaving the depot. The motorcades and Secret Service men, that are necessary for the President and Vice President, seem incongruous on the sleepy streets of a town like Plains. (Neyland)

be serious, and Gloria thought she would be out of the hospital that night or the next morning. I was to go ahead and set up the Christmas tree before driving in to the hospital in Americus.

The Carters have their own tradition about Christmas trees—a tradition that fits their concern for conservation. They select the scrawniest, least healthy trees to cut and place in their homes, leaving the hardier trees to grow in the forests. I was not aware of this tradition and I was completely dismayed when confronted by Miss Lillian's tree. What I found in the carport was a pathetic collection of branches that looked as if it had been lobbed off a finer tree.

When I took it inside and struggled to get it into the tree-stand, all the branches were on one side, and most of them were near the bottom. To make matters worse, the trunk bent and twisted in three different directions. After working at it for over an hour, trimming off one branch after another, I had it standing. But there wasn't much left of it.

Later, at the hospital, I tactlessly suggested to Billy and Sybil, "You really ought to get her another tree; that's the ugliest Christmas tree I've ever seen." Billy nodded politely and promised to take care of it. His response was typically kind and very considerate of my feelings. This concern for others is a side of his personality that is not generally seen by the public. He may be a "good ol' boy," enjoying his fun, but he is not the beer-drinking buffoon

Below: **Jimmy, like the experienced father he is, holds Earl.** (Neyland)

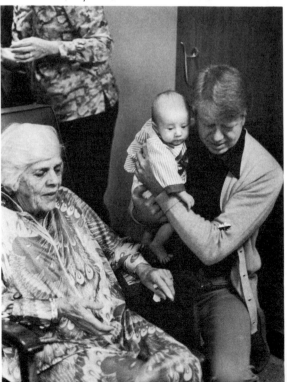

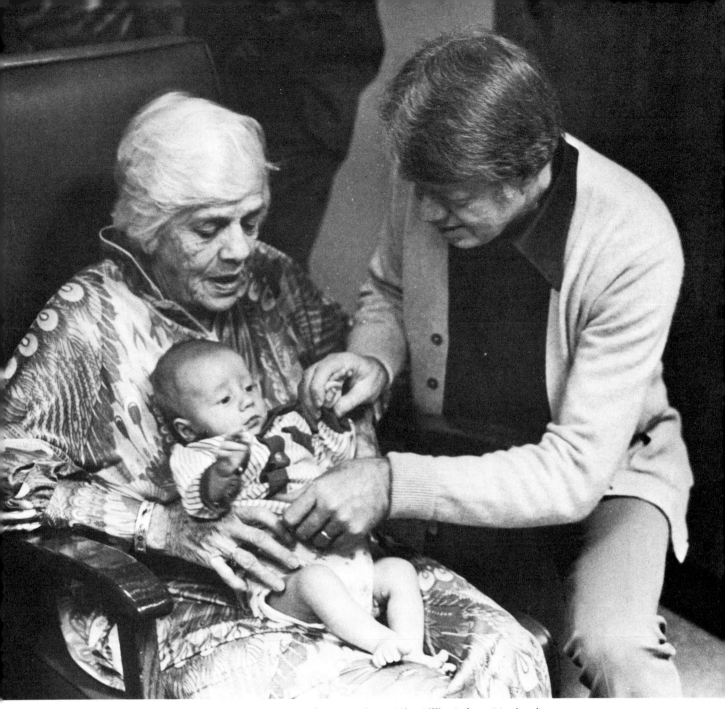

Jimmy Carter reaches out to take his nephew, Earl Carter, from Miss Lillian's lap. (Neyland)

that some members of the press have made him out to be. When friends or family are in need, Billy is first on the scene.

In that respect, Sybil Carter is very much like her husband. When Miss Lillian needs help, she does not usually call on her sons; she calls on Sybil—or Gloria.

Billy and Sybil together manage the Peanut Warehouse, operating it very much in the same kind of husband/wife partner-

ship that Jimmy and Rosalynn began some years ago. Sybil doesn't look like a businesswoman, but, since her marriage to Billy at age sixteen, she has become a true Carter, developing her talents to the fullest while maintaining her role as a wife and the mother of six children.

With Christmas only two days away, Miss Lillian was, understandably, not overjoyed at being in the hospital. Traditional-

Miss Lillian holding her grandson Earl. Behind her are Sybil and Billy Carter. By her side is Rosalynn. (Neyland)

Rosalynn tells Gloria about the photo album. Jimmy, his back to the camera, talks to Caron. Amy reads. Miss Lillian holds Earl, and Sybil talks to Billy in the other room. (Neyland)

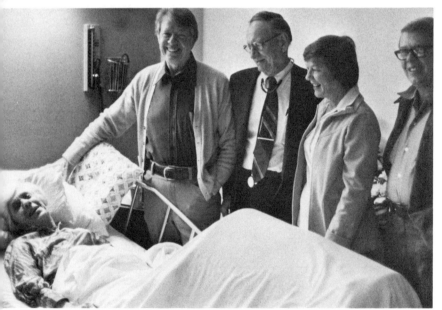

Family and family doctor at Miss Lillian's bedside on Christmas day. Left to right: Jimmy Carter, Dr. John Robinson, Gloria Carter Spann, and Billy Carter. (Neyland)

Right: Rosalynn Carter at Miss Lillian's bedside on Christmas day. The two women have been extremely close since Rosalynn was a small child, and both have grown weary of the rumors and questions concerning a rift between them. There has never been any serious dispute between the two. (Neyland)

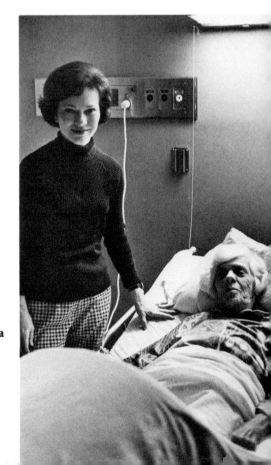

ly, the entire Carter family gathered at her house for breakfast; and she was eager that this Christmas be no different. But her doctor prescribed rest, and it was not likely that she would rest while cooking breakfast for twenty people.

At the hospital, I got to know Gloria better. We laughed and joked a lot and spoke seriously, too. Miss Lillian had told me that, like Billy, Gloria had broken with the church years ago, disapproving of the hypocrisy she found there. But Gloria is deeply religious in her own way, living her philosophy while refusing to be bound by church strictures.

At the hospital, I also met Ruth, who flew in from North Carolina to visit her mother. From the moment she entered the room, her energy reverberated everywhere, and the laughter and talk doubled in volume and enjoyment. No,

Amy Carter inspects a new paint set she received for Christmas. (Neyland)

Chip Carter with his father. (Neyland)

the "faith healer" daughter didn't lay hands on her mother or command her to rise and walk. But her presence certainly did make her mother smile oftener.

Of course, some of the grandchildren came to visit, too. Jeff and his wife, Annette, came for a while, bringing photos he had taken on St. Simon's Island off the Georgia coast. Kim, Billy's oldest daughter, who studies speech at Georgia Southwestern while working as an announcer for a local radio station, brightened the room with her exuberant, pretty face. Kim, Miss Lillian admits, was always her favorite

Brother and sister: Chip listens to a family conversation while Amy reads one of the Nancy Drew mysteries she received for Christmas. (Neyland)

Jimmy and Billy. (Neyland)

Gloria removes a label from a jacket that Jimmy received for Christmas. (Neyland)

grandchild until Amy came along. Jana, Billy's second daughter, is an even greater bundle of energy; and Buddy, Billy's older son, is quiet, sensitive, reflective, and respectful.

On Christmas Day, the hospital relaxed its rule about children, so that the younger grandchildren could be with Miss Lillian. Just as each of Miss Lillian's children is distinctly different, so are these grandchildren distinct individuals. Billy's daughter Marle appears to be shy, though she is reputed to be mischievous occasionally. Nine-year-old Mandy is bouncy and energetic. Amy is somewhat more serious, with fits of enthusiasm, and infant Earl is amazingly well behaved, considering all the different Carters who reach out to hold him.

Christmas Day with the Carters is like a family Christmas anywhere in the country. There are laughter, shrieks of delight from the children, thank-yous, and exclamations from the adults. The Carters exchange practical gifts, with a few toys and books for the younger children.

But because this Christmas was being celebrated in a hospital room, and partly

Rosalynn, Gloria, and Jimmy get a few laughs out of old family photos in one of the albums Rosalynn had made up as Christmas gifts for each of the families. (Neyland)

Rosalynn holding Earl Carter, with Christmas gifts scattered about the sofa. (Neyland)

because it was the last one that Jimmy and Rosalynn would spend as private citizens, for at least four years, it was special. And, in the midst of it all, Miss Lillian was glowing like a candle.

After the family had gone, each to its separate home, and after the nurse had brought in her breakfast, Miss Lillian concluded, "It's been the happiest Christmas I've spent in years." And then she laughed. "And I don't have all those dishes to wash."

For Jimmy and Rosalynn Carter, Christmas was perhaps the last personal family celebration. Less than a month later, Jimmy Carter was inaugurated as the thirty-ninth president of the United States.

The inauguration of 1977 was very special and very different. Beginning with the inaugural invitations, Jimmy set a tone of economy and conservation. The invitations were printed, rather than engraved, and they were on recycled paper. Those who wanted seats for the ceremonies, and those who wanted to attend the concert and the balls, had to pay only a nominal fee. Drinks cost extra. Black tie was optional.

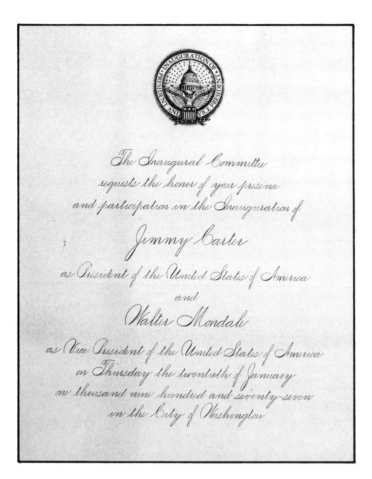

The Inaugural Committee
requests the honor of your presence
and participation in the Inauguration of

Jimmy Carter

as President of the United States of America
and

Walter Mondale

as Vice President of the United States of America
on Thursday the twentieth of January
one thousand nine hundred and seventy-seven
in the City of Washington

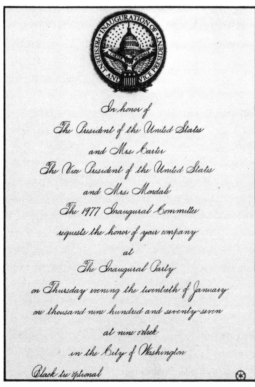

In honor of
The President of the United States
and Mrs. Carter
The Vice President of the United States
and Mrs. Mondale
The 1977 Inaugural Committee
requests the honor of your company
at
The Inaugural Party
on Thursday evening the twentieth of January
one thousand nine hundred and seventy-seven
at nine o'clock
in the City of Washington
Black tie optional

Jimmy cut down on the actual ceremonies too. There were fewer and shorter prayers, and his inaugural address was brief and to the point. The theme of his address was "a new spirit," and as demonstrated by his words and his later actions, that new spirit was one of forgiveness and healing, hard work and mutual cooperation, unity and trust. But perhaps most important, he returned the American government to the American people:

You have given me a great responsibility—to stay close to you, to be worthy of you, and to exemplify what you are. Let us create together a new national spirit of unity and trust. Your strength can compensate for my weakness and your wisdom can help to minimize my mistakes.

Let us learn together and laugh together and work together and pray together, confident that in the end we will triumph together in the right.

The American dream endures. We must once again have full faith in our country—and in one another.

And then, in an act that spoke more loudly than the words, with a gesture unprecedented in American history, Jimmy Carter showed that he trusted the American people: He chose to walk from the Capitol Building all the way to the White House. The people cheered, and many eyes were moist; Jimmy had acknowledged that he was a man of the people, and that he would endeavor to remain close to the people. The people were placing their trust in him, and he was willing to trust them.

The inaugural party that night drew the biggest crowd ever at the Armory. Men in sports jackets rubbed elbows with women in elegant, expensive gowns; men in tuxedos danced with women in pants suits—when there was room to dance. Most of the time, people were wedged in so tightly there was hardly room to walk. One guest commented good-humoredly,

Jimmy Carter is sworn into the office of president of the United States by Chief Justice Warren Burger, while Rosalynn looks on. (Wide World)

"I know Jimmy promised to bring us together, but this is ridiculous."

I was there that night, in a plain suit, sitting among the Carters and the Smiths, the mothers, the children, the grandchildren, and the cousins.

A sentimental occasion it may have been, but it spoke genuinely of the manner in which Jimmy Carter was to begin his term of office. His first official act was to pardon draft resisters of the Vietnam War. A few days later he announced his intention of creating a job program that would emphasize employment for Vietnam veterans. He initiated a program of energy conservation that was entirely dependent upon the cooperation of the American people. And he sent his Vice President off to Europe to attempt to rebuild the fading relations with American allies.

To maintain his closeness to the people, Jimmy reinstituted the "fireside chats" Franklin Roosevelt had used so effectively, and he planned a nationwide telephone call-in program to listen to the opinions of American citizens.

He does not expect everyone in the nation to agree with him; in fact, he appreciates differences of opinion. He knows that those differences are essential to the workings of American democracy. Personal individuality is the greatest expression of American freedom; Jimmy Carter knows that, because it is the way he grew up as a member of the Carter family. The greatest wounds to the American spirit have been created by those who would attempt to make all the people conform to a single attitude. These are the wounds that Jimmy Carter—and all the distinctly individual members of the Carter family—are concerned about healing.

Miss Lillian's dog, Periwinkle. (Neyland)

The Pond House. (Neyland)

Mother and daughter—Miss Lillian with Gloria Carter Spann. (Neyland)

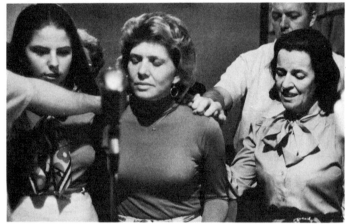

Ruth Carter Stapleton—the "faith healer" at work. (*Newsweek*—Jeff Lowenthal)

Miss Lillian and Gloria, with Gloria's dogs, Charlie and Forty. (Neyland)